BUSES
YEARBOOK 2000

Edited by
STEWART J. BROWN

Ian Allan
PUBLISHING

First published 1999

ISBN 0 7110 2673 4

Published by Ian Allan Publishing

an imprint of Ian Allan Publishing Ltd, Terminal House, Shepperton, Surrey TW17 8AS. Printed by Ian Allan Printing Ltd, Riverdene Business Park, Hersham, Surrey KT12 4RG.

Code: 9908/F

Front cover:
Wilts & Dorset operate the largest fleet of Optare Spectras. Here on a glorious June day, No 3128 (L128 ELJ) makes its way through Bournemouth to the terminus of route 123 at the Triangle. *Philip Lamb*

Back cover, top:
Stuart's of Manchester bought a variety of second-hand buses, many with Scottish ancestry. The point is made by an ex-Strathclyde Atlantean in Manchester's Piccadilly bus station. *Stewart J. Brown*

Back cover, bottom:
The Dennis Dart, most often with Plaxton Pointer body, is the new face of London's transport. This is a Thamesway bus with FirstBus logo in 1996. Now the First name takes precedence over the company name. *Peter Rowlands*

Title page:
Pictured on Stockton High Street in 1985 is a Northern Counties re-bodied 1970 Atlantean, one of a number operated by Cleveland Transit at that time. *Kevin Lane*

Contents

OF *BAYS* AND *BUSTLES*

Gavin Booth charts some of the high-points and the low-points of body design for rear-engined double-deckers.

Above:
'Some might argue that the RT design was never surpassed...' An RT basks in the sun at Victoria bus station in the early 1960s. SJB

Below:
As the 1960s progressed, so designs became more adventurous. Alexander produced one of the most stylish early bodies for Atlanteans and Fleetlines. Full-height models had deeper windows on the lower deck. Lowheight bodies, as on this Western Scottish Fleetline, had equal-depth windows on both decks. The attractive curved windscreens were a distinctive feature, although some operators specified flat glass to cut replacement costs. SJB

You can almost imagine the discussion. Representatives from the bodybuilders are sitting down with the chief engineer of a major bus company, working out how the first rear-engined double-deckers might look. A bus is just a box after all, the engineer might say. The traffic people want as many seats as possible, so we use every last inch of the 30ft length and 8ft width we have to play with for internal body space. That means there's no need for fancy curves, which is fine by me — flat metal, flat glass is what I need; easy to repair. Who really cares what the buses *look* like? They're new, they're different, they're big — surely they don't need to be pretty as well?

The bodybuilders would then take up the cause enthusiastically. Flat panels and flat glass are fine by us, they might say, and at little or no extra cost we can adapt designs that we developed for front-engined deckers.

Unfair? Maybe, but when the first rear-engined double-deckers started to take to the streets just 40 years ago there was a sense of disappointment among those of us who cared about such things, that a great opportunity had been missed to take bus design forward. I suppose we should have realised that these things can take time.

Look at the first recognisably 'modern' double-decker, the Leyland Titan TD1 of 1927. A classic, certainly, but a design that was quirky and soon looked outdated as bodybuilders got to grips with new materials and building techniques. Barely 10 years later builders like Leyland, Metro-Cammell and Roe were producing designs that represented a giant leap forward, culminating in London Transport's timeless 1939 design for its RT class. Some might argue that the RT design was never surpassed and that nothing built over the next 30 years came close.

Maybe, then, the rear-engined double-decker had to wait at least 10 years before somebody came up with a classic design. Fortunately, we didn't have to wait too long.

But back to the beginning. Leyland, it must be said, always had a good feel for how buses should look. While it had its own in-house bodybuilding plant, this was controllable, and even when it worked with outside builders, most notably Metro-Cammell on joint projects like the integral single-deck Olympic, you had the feeling that the final appearance of the bus owed much to Leyland's influence, particularly when all of Leyland's input, barring the wheels, was tucked away out of sight, and there wasn't even a radiator to declare its parentage.

So it surely was with the prototype Leyland Atlantean, the legendary 281 ATC, an integral rear-engined double-decker developed by Leyland and Metro-Cammell in 1956. Here was a sleek, unquestionably modern bus, with a true lowheight (13ft 3in) body that boasted clean, balanced lines. So it was a surprise, to put it mildly, when the first production Atlanteans were shown in 1958, and turned out to be a compromise between 281 ATC and MCW's familiar, but widely criticised, Orion design with its unequal-depth side windows. Even Alexander, which built one of the production prototypes, appeared to have emulated the Orion, but saved the day with some more heavily-radiused windows.

These buses set the pattern for the first few years of Atlantean production, and when Daimler followed with the first rear-engined Fleetlines from 1960, these were little different. In some liveries these buses could look impressive, but they often looked slab-sided and overbearing.

So what happened to change all that? Somebody, somewhere recognised that rear-engined double-deckers were a totally different breed. It may have been the bodybuilders, who took one look at the new Atlanteans or Fleetlines leaving their factory gates, and realised that they could do much better.

Maybe.

Or, more likely, it was the operators, wanting something rather more attractive for their passengers. At first they had been wary of the rear-engined double-decker, and bought only small batches to see if they were really what was wanted. Once they had made up their minds, there was then the question of what the buses should *look* like. Municipal pride was important in those pre-PTE days, and it was the big corporation fleets that used their buying muscle to persuade bodybuilders to supply something considerably more inspiring than the early bodies.

And the first thing they looked at was...

Top right:
'...these buses could look impressive, but they often looked slab-sided...' An early Atlantean with Metro-Cammell body in the Birmingham City Transport fleet. The use of deep windows on the lower deck was a feature of Metro-Cammell's contemporary Orion design. This 1960 bus was originally a Leyland demonstrator, hence the Lancashire registration. Alan Broughall

Above right:
'Liverpool and MCW developed an impressive design...' On the left, a peaked dome and polished trim mark one of Liverpool's new Atlanteans. The fleet's original trial Atlantean passes, showing points of difference. SJB

Opposite:
Room had to be provided at the rear for the engine cover to be raised — which it often was. SJB

..The Bustle

What Leyland and Daimler gave the bodybuilders to play with was a bare chassis with the engine mounted in a compartment at the rear. This was a new experience for them; normally they had a chassis with an engine at the front, with a radiator or tin front to work around. These provided the bus with its 'personality', something a bustle at the back could never do.

It took bodybuilders some time to come to terms with the rear-mounted engine compartment. The straightforward approach was to accept that the engine was there, and make no attempt to disguise it. Because early engine compartments had to be raised in their entirety to give access to the engine, space had to be allowed above. This led to the notch-back appearance of so many earlier rear-engined double-deckers. Right from the start, Northern Counties got round this by fitting out-swinging corner panels at lower deck window level, which gave an unbroken side profile. Other builders adopted similar ploys, and the chassis manufacturers soon responded with three-part engine compartment doors that lifted only in the centre section; the corners were designed to open out for easier access.

Many of the bespoke designs went for smooth rear ends, but the bodybuilders' standard designs still included the cutaway right to the end of Atlantean and Fleetline production.

It is difficult to pinpoint the end of the bustle, but it was probably around 1984 when the last Atlanteans were placed in service. All later models, from the Bristol VRT onwards, have been designed to avoid the bustle effect, by incorporating the engine compartment into the body structure.

After the bodybuilders came to terms with the back end of rear-engined double-deckers, they started to think about...

...The Front End

The Atlantean and Fleetline had radiators at the rear, so the designers sat down with a blank sheet of paper when considering the front end. Looking at some of the early Atlanteans, it is tempting to suggest that they simply passed the blank sheet of paper to the coachbuilders. The front ends had windows, destination screens, side and head lamps, registration number and, er, that's it.

It took a late 1950s change in Construction & Use regulations to help things along. No longer was it necessary for the driver's windscreen to open, and this, coupled with advances in glass-fibre technology, allowed designers a much freer rein.

Now many of the buses that were taking to the streets were undeniably modern, and looked efficient and suited to their purpose, just like the legions of private cars that were attracting more and more passengers away from public transport. Bus operators scratched their heads and looked at ways of stopping the rot. Bigger buses, fewer of them, seemed like one answer. Maybe they could save more money by doing away with conductors, and from 1966 driver-only operation of double-deckers was legalised.

But some operators recognised that looks played their part in attracting passengers, and if the bodybuilders seemed reluctant to supply designs that offered much in the way of dramatic styling, then the operators would flex their muscles and persuade them to rethink.

So Glasgow and Alexander came up with a style boasting much glass-fibre and curved glass; Liverpool and MCW developed an impressive design that used angles and peaks to good effect; Oldham and Sunderland added peaks to Roe bodies; Bolton worked with East Lancs to come up with a big-windowed design that was a foretaste of greater things from Manchester; Sheffield took the uninspiring Park Royal standard and improved it greatly

DKC 370L

1370

with a new front end and Birmingham adopted something similar — and suddenly better-looking double-deckers were the order of the day.

Probably the most dramatic of the new designs was Manchester Corporation's 1968 Mancunian, designed as a one-man double-decker, and built by several builders. This crisp, simple body was a milestone in double-deck design and paved the way for the SELNEC Standards, which were among the best-conceived double-deckers of the 1970s.

It was undeniable that a simple facelift could dramatically improve the appearance of this new breed of double-decker, and some amazingly bland designs were transformed in this way. Some builders took the easy option and replicated the more successful designs — like the Alexander-lookalike front ends produced by MCW, Northern Counties and Roe — but gradually there appeared to be a new awareness of looks.

Right:
Rear engines in Sheffield. The approaching Fleetline has an attractive East Lancs body using — by the standards of the day — unusually deep windows. SJB

Below:
The idea of concealing the bustle was pioneered by Northern Counties and soon copied by other builders. This artist's impression of a Roe body for Leeds City Transport shows how it improved the rear profile. SJB collection

Above:
Nottingham developed a distinctive style which was modified over the years but never lost the basic Nottingham look. The bodies were built by East Lancs and Northern Counties and fitted in the main to Fleetline and Atlantean chassis. Unusual features were a stout bumper, a single-width entrance door on later, dual-door, buses, and a straight staircase. Careful positioning of the seats allowed up to 78 to be fitted to buses which were 9.5m long and had two doors — at a time when comparable single-door buses in other fleets were unlikely to seat more than 75. SJB

Top left:
From the outset, the ECW-bodied Bristol VRT was designed with a flush rear end, effectively bringing the engine into the lower saloon. Early ECW bodies had flat glass windscreens; later examples, such as this Cheltenham District bus, used the double-curvature BET screen to improve the frontal appearance. SJB

Left:
'...the tinsmith was simply left to cut a hole in the front panel...' Not all bodybuilders coped with the front-mounted radiator of the Bristol VRT with the panache of ECW. An East Lancs-bodied VRT of the Merseyside PTE shows the simple style adopted for the front grille. SJB

Bottom left:
Most 1970s designs used fewer, bigger, side windows. London Transport's Fleetlines were bodied by MCW and Park Royal to this design, utilising a curved windscreen which had previously been seen on LT single-deck designs of the 1960s. The only other buyer of this style of body was the South Yorkshire PTE. SJB

When Bristol introduced the VRT chassis in 1968 it incorporated a front-mounted radiator, which provided body designers with a new challenge. With Eastern Coach Works bodywork, by far the most popular combination, the VRT sported a bold grille similar to that on other Bristol/ECW products. For other coachbuilders the front-mounted radiator proved to be a bit of a nuisance, and you had the impression that the tinsmith was simply left to cut a hole in the front panel and fit a metal mesh behind this.

Subsequent rear-engined chassis also had front-mounted radiators, which meant that more bodybuilders had to tackle that hole in the front panel. Some never seemed quite sure what to do; others went for the bold approach, with large and distinctive grilles. Leyland and MCW contrived designs that incorporated grilles into neat front-end treatments.

When MCW responded to the threat of Leyland's double-deck monopoly with the Scania-based Metropolitan model in 1973, it moved away from the traditional approach to windscreen design with an asymmetric two-piece screen, deeper on the nearside. The later MCW Metrobus had a more restrained version of this screen, but the Mark II Metrobus returned to a more conventional treatment. The value of the asymmetric screens was always doubtful, but they did act as a means of easy recognition.

It took a new builder to break the mould. Optare had been set up to continue the bus building activities abandoned by Leyland when it closed the Charles H. Roe business at Leeds. It had started by building Roe-like bodies on Leyland Olympian, but quickly started to develop a range of impressive designs that caused its rivals to sit up and take notice. Its 1991 Spectra body, mounted on DAF DB250 chassis, introduced a softer, more rounded look, and took double-deck body design forward. Northern Counties and Alexander quickly recognised that the softer look worked, and came up with the up-market Palatine II and Royale models, offered as more expensive options to the Palatine I and R-type bodies.

East Lancs, when it was a smaller-league builder specialising in small batches on varied chassis for the municipal market, suddenly discovered style in the 1990s, and in 1996 introduced the strikingly angular Cityzen body. Within a year this had become the Pyoneer, continuing the East Lancs 'Y' theme, with a softer front end that shared common styling with its single-deck designs. One of the most innovative features on the Cityzen was the destination box, which formed part of the front-end styling, appearing as a continuation of the upper deck front screen, rather than looking as if it had been tacked on afterwards. East Lancs' low-floor Lolyne has similar frontal styling.

Other builders took up this theme with their bodies for low-floor double-deckers, and these will become increasingly familiar in the next few years. The Alexander ALX400 (and three-axle ALX500) designs are obviously part of the ALX family, sharing common front-panel styling with single-deck models. The Plaxton President, built at the former Northern Counties plant at Wigan, is another totally new design, with a softly-styled front end and deep side windows.

So the truth had finally dawned: it didn't really matter what the rest of the body looked like — as long as the front was OK, who was going to worry?

Except there was the vexed question of how many windows there should be on the sides.

Two-bay or Not Two-bay

That was the question. Well, not *two*-bay as such, but it would have spoiled the heading.

Before we consider the vexed question of the number of bays, we must consider the equally vexed question of just what *is* a bay. In the days of front-engined/rear entrance buses it was easy: how many windows were there between the lower deck bulkheads? So a Routemaster, for example, has a four-bay body.

It was less easy to apply this logic to rear-engined double-deckers, and there are different schools of thought. I favour the upper deck solution, so the early Atlanteans had seven-bay bodies, which took their

Below:
'It took a new builder to break the mould.'
Optare's trend-setting Spectra, in operation with
Reading Buses in London. Reading was the first
customer for the Spectra. SJB

approach to window spacing from their front-engined predecessors. But that made window alignment a bit of a problem, so from 1969 Park Royal, and eventually other builders, went for a four-and-a-half bay body, with the half-bay aligning with the engine compartment. The pillar spacing gave good, big windows, and many major fleets went for this layout — most notably Birmingham, London and Manchester.

Not that every builder slavishly followed the four-and-a-half bay rule. Alexander and East Lancs, for example, stuck to seven-bay bodies, and ECW went it alone with a distinguished, if dated, six-and-a-half bay style, that clearly dated back to its Lodekka bodies.

But just when it looked that the four-and-a-half bay body might become universal, MCW challenged conventional wisdom with its Metropolitan body in 1973. This introduced a six-bay layout, with almost equal-length windows, and within a few years this was the accepted layout on models like the Leyland Titan and MCW Metrobus, as well as on the new body designs produced for the Leyland Olympian chassis from 1980 onwards. Two of the most familiar Olympian bodies, from Alexander and ECW/Roe, were six-bay designs, and addressed the problem of longer Olympians with a short window bay in the centre of the body, in the way that Park Royal lengthened the Routemaster without affecting too many standard parts.

The more recent moves to bonded glazing and square-edged gasket glazing, together with the fashion for matt black window pillars, have all rather muddied the waters. Bay lengths are less obvious these days when the side view often gives an impression of continuous window.

With low-floor double-deckers the trend is towards buses that appear to have the maximum window sizes, none more so than the East Lancs Lolyne, which has a six-and-a-half bay layout on a body that is 10.55m long and from the side appears to be all window.

Opposite:
Alexander's Royale took the company's standard R-type structure and added square-cornered glazing and deep curved windscreens. FirstGroup operates Royales in Edinburgh, Glasgow, Leeds and Manchester. This is an SMT bus. All Royales are on Volvo Olympian chassis. Alexander

Below:
East Lancs shook off a generation of bland designs with the Cityzen and associated models, including the Pyoneer seen here on a 1998 Dennis Arrow operated by Capital Citybus. SJB

Above:
The new look has been carried on to new low-floor models. Representing the style we'll be seeing more of in the new millennium is one of the first Alexander ALX400s, for Arriva London North. The chassis is a DAF DB250LF. Alexander

So standardisation rules the day. Gradually the shrinking number of double-deck bodybuilders managed to resist the overtures of the operators who wanted something different, and instead chose to provide highly-standardised designs that offer little chance for personalised bodies. Today, individuality is catered for by stylish liveries and by creating an attractive environment for passengers, as FirstGroup has demonstrated with its 'Barbie' livery and distinctive interior decor.

And passengers, it must be said, have not always fared as well as they might at the hands of bodybuilders and bus operators. Today, arguably, they've never had it so good.

SHETLAND
SOJOURNS

In the 1950s and 1960s Shetland operators ran an amazing selection of buses. **Roy Marshall** visited the islands in 1957 and 1964.

Below:
Something of the remoteness of Shetland can be gathered from this 1964 view of a Duple-bodied Bedford SB crossing the treeless landscape. It was operated by Leask of Lerwick.
All photographs in this article by the author

Inset:
Prewar buses were still commonplace in 1957 and included this Duple-bodied Bedford WTB operated by Leslie of Virkie on a service from Lerwick to Sumburgh five days a week. A postwar Bedford/Duple stands behind. Sumburgh lies at the southern tip of mainland Shetland.

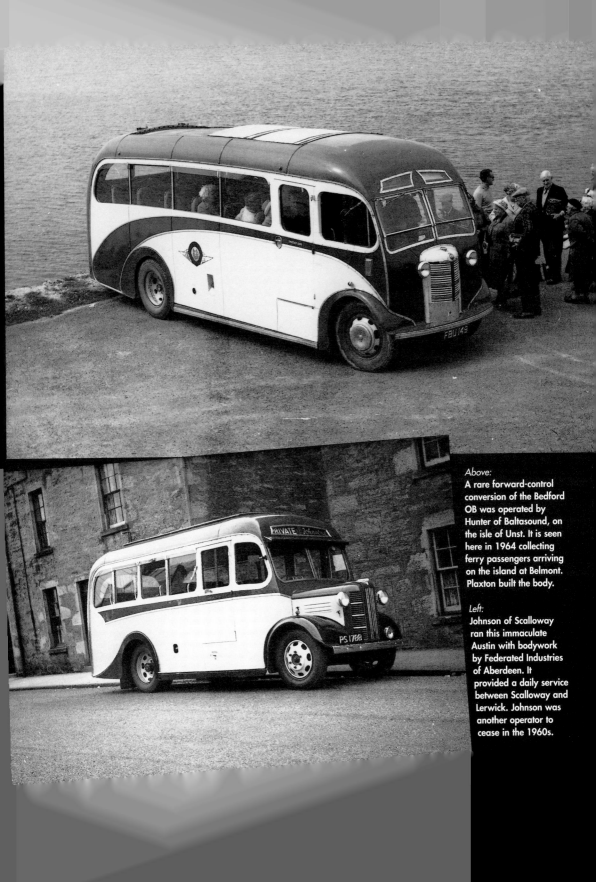

Above:
A rare forward-control conversion of the Bedford OB was operated by Hunter of Baltasound, on the isle of Unst. It is seen here in 1964 collecting ferry passengers arriving on the island at Belmont. Plaxton built the body.

Left:
Johnson of Scalloway ran this immaculate Austin with bodywork by Federated Industries of Aberdeen. It provided a daily service between Scalloway and Lerwick. Johnson was another operator to cease in the 1960s.

Right:
This unlikely-looking vehicle was a seven-seat bus, although the passengers clearly didn't enjoy the best of views. It is a Morris-Commercial of Leslie of Sandsound and is seen in Lerwick in 1964. Leslie ran the post office and general store at Sandsound and the Morris-Commercial served as both van and bus.

Below:
Jamieson of Cullivoe — still running coaches four decades on — had this Kenex-bodied Austin K-series providing its Cullivoe to Mid Yell route in 1957.

Above:
A rather more conventional Morris-Commercial coach operating Leask's Lerwick town service in 1957. It has a Churchill body.

Left:
Austins were a common choice on the Shetland Isles, the biggest model being the CXB. Leask of Lerwick operated this one, also with bodywork by Churchill of Norwich. The grille is similar to that used on Austin cars of the early 1950s — albeit considerably bigger.

Austin built K-series goods chassis during World War 2, a small number of which formed the basis of buses in the north of Scotland. This austere-looking example belonged to Manson of West Sandwick, on the island of Yell.

Right:
A classic minibus? This impressive 1937 Dodge was owned by Sinclair of Melby and was a seven-seater complete with roof rack for luggage. Sinclair's operation came to an end in 1961.

Above:
Samlesbury coach bodies were fairly rare. This one, on an Austin CXB, was operated by Georgeson & Moore of Scalloway. Like most PSVs in the Shetlands it was petrol-engined. This is a 1964 view.

Left:
Modernity in the 1960s with a Kenex-bodied Austin belonging to Williamson of Gruting. The swept side mouldings hark back to an earlier era, as does the Duple-bodied Bedford OB alongside, which belonged to Watt of Reawick.

The TV programmes you talked about on the bus — or were they the unbelievable buses you discussed in front of the telly? Oliver Howarth flickers gently in the corner as he looks back over four decades starting here with those 'swingin sixties'.

Tellygraphic Memory
'I'll get you, Butler!'

Hero of the Industry
Ralph Bennett, who brought elegant and passenger-friendly vehicles to Bolton and Manchester and set design trends which lasted well into the 1980s.

Till Death Us Do Part
There is a view that the PD3 was indestructible and some operators agreed with this to the point of eschewing anything more modern. But at root it was a 1940s bus sitting uneasily in the swinging sixties; engineering departments certainly found it predictable but passengers in Stockport in 1969 must have compared their latest rear entrance PD3s with Manchester's sexy new Mancunians and despaired of its bellowing, uncouth behaviour. A lot were withdrawn after less than 12 years — cheap to maintain but embarrassing and expensive to staff.

The Sky's The Limit
The Atlantean started as an oddity but, in the way of the industry, was bought because it was fashionable to have. Its quiet, smooth ride was a delight compared with other vehicles at a time when listening to music on headphones on a bus was only a dream (even if it would later become a nightmare). By 1964 it was clear that one-man operation was on its way and the big municipalities started to buy the Atlanteans, foreseeing that here was the quick way to save money and make scarce staff go further. So far as the salesmen were concerned, the Sky was the limit.

The Prisoner
Dennis Loline was The Prisoner but what was Aldershot & District Number 1? The Loline was probably a good bus — but no one ever did find out whose side it was on, as its captors constantly changed tactics to make sure the Loline could not escape captivity in the enclosed world of A…

Crossroads
Will Meg ever discontinue the FS? Will Benny get the VRL running in time for Central SMT? Will anybody persuade Ulsterbus to buy a standee single-decker? Will the public realise that Bristol is embroiled in a soap opera and coming to a crossroads — innovation or reliability? Tune in next time to find out.

The Likely Lads
Well, whatever did happen to the Panther and Panther Cub? Certainly the Panther Cub was a bad mistake, spending its time lazing in workshops and never doing a proper day's work. But the Panther had the right attitude; it was smart, quiet, well presented, wore the right badges. Such a shame that things didn't work out.

The Saint
Even though it tended to genuflect in icy conditions, the swashbuckling RE was held in awe by a lot of hard-to-impress fleet engineers and long after other types had fallen apart, obsolete REs continued to wear their ring of confidence.

Never Mind The Quality
Daimler's sales figures were transformed by the Fleetline's arrival — a reliable, Gardner-engined, lowheight Atlantean was just what a lot of people wanted, particularly as the manufacturer was happy to make Fleetlines to measure. You can have an off-the-peg 30ft or 33ft or we could run you up a little 28ft model, sir; full-height, lowheight, one deck or two — never mind the quality (it's fine) — feel the length.

Going For A Song
But the Seddon RU would put an end to the fleet engineer's carefree whistling in any season.

GLE EYED
1: *1960s*

Individuality Is In

1960s bus operators are looking for greater carrying capacity and simpler, more reliable vehicles.

Below:
NEVER MIND THE QUALITY:
Birmingham and the West Midlands PTE were big users of Daimler's evergreen Fleetline. A late MCW-bodied example climbs Digbeth High Street in 1984.

Above:
THE SAINT:
Still pulling the girls (and boys) is this East Yorkshire open-top RE, super-cool in Scarborough.
All photographs by the author

WILTS &

Michael H. C. Baker charts the decline and rise of a well-known South Coast name.

Mention Wilts & Dorset and immediately we're into an identity crisis. It was all the fault of Adolf Hitler, for it was one of his doodlebugs which, landing on the house at the bottom of our garden in Thornton Heath, removed our roof and windows and us to Bournemouth and so introduced me to the Wilts & Dorset bus company. Except that in those days it was Hants & Dorset. Except that there was Wilts & Dorset too; but only marginally. Let me explain.

In the 1940s any buses in the Bournemouth area which weren't painted yellow, and which were not trolleybuses, were likely to be green Hants & Dorset vehicles. The only Wilts & Dorset ones I can remember were ancient open staircase TD1 Titans which ran to Salisbury.

As Bournemouth was in Hampshire and our weekly excursion to visit my grandmother and aunt and uncle in Poole meant crossing the Dorset border at County Gates we naturally enough took a Hants & Dorset double-decker. You can still do the journey today, but the whole of it will be in Dorset, your bus is more likely to be a single-decker, it will be painted red and it will belong to Wilts & Dorset.

What happened was this. Wilts & Dorset and Hants & Dorset were once quite separate companies within the great Tilling empire and went their separate ways, the former in red, the latter in green. Then in 1964 a joint general manager was appointed and a year later the Wilts & Dorset registered office was transferred from Salisbury to Bournemouth, so when the National Bus Company assumed control of both, it was generally expected that the two would become one. Which is precisely what happened and the merged company became Hants & Dorset although, rather surprisingly, poppy red was chosen for the livery rather than leaf green.

In 1983, with the break-up and privatisation of NBC, Hants & Dorset was divided three ways. Fareham-based Provincial, which had also been absorbed by Hants & Dorset, reappeared, whilst the eastern section of the main company became Hampshire Bus. This left the section from the New Forest westwards as the third element and it was decided that it would revive the Wilts & Dorset fleetname. Let's hope that all is now clear. And let me add one final piece of clear blue sky in the top left-hand

corner of the jigsaw by reminding readers that in the boundary changes of the early 1970s, Bournemouth was removed kicking and screaming from Hampshire into Dorset. Great was the rejoicing in 1997 when, whilst still geographically and postally in Dorset, Bournemouth became a unitary authority and took charge of its own affairs.

A management team consisting of managing and finance director Hugh Malone, operations manager Andrew Bryce and engineering director Rodney Luxton bought Wilts & Dorset from NBC. Andrew Bryce told me that he had plenty of experience of being an area manager of a large concern where all the important decisions were taken far away and he has no wish to go back to that situation. So we may assume that Wilts & Dorset's attractive livery of red with stylish black and

DORSET

white stripes and an equally stylish fleet name is going to remain; style was to become the keyword of the company in relation to its vehicles too.

I spoke to Andrew Bryce at the end of 1998 and we discussed the close relationship Wilts & Dorset has developed with Optare in the 1990s, for it is this which has resulted in a remarkably up-to-date fleet of highly individual buses.

Let us start in 1998 and work our way backwards. On 26 August 1998 a most unusual sight met shoppers and tourists at Salisbury Market Square, for on display was the city's new fleet of three Spectra low-floor double-deckers and 16 Solos. For years controversy had raged in the city around proposals for a bypass cutting across the water meadows and ruining one of the most famous views in the country, that which Constable painted looking

Opposite:
The modern face of Wilts & Dorset. An Optare Spectra heads through Studland village in 1997.
All photographs by the author

Top:
Wilts & Dorset was one of the first operators to place large orders for the Optare Solo. One leaves Bournemouth for Poole in October 1998.

Above:
DAFs figure in both the bus and coach operations. A Plaxton-bodied SB3000 arrives in Bath from Salisbury.

towards the cathedral. In 1998 the Government announced that the bypass would not be built. Wilts & Dorset decided that it was time to invest £2 million to provide Salisbury city services with a completely low-floor fleet — a nationwide first, as Andrew Bryce, not without a justifiable touch of pride, was quick to point out.

He added that the Government, having had the courage to make the decision on the bypass, then got cold feet and said there would need to be another two years to study the whole issue of traffic in and around Salisbury. Which meant that not a penny of public money has been available to provide the infrastructure to go with Salisbury's splendid new buses.

The Solo is a remarkable vehicle which Optare has produced with the close co-operation of Wilts & Dorset. The company had no interest in the uncomfortable bread vans which passed as PSVs in the early days of minibuses. Instead it invested in a large fleet of Metroriders, marketed as Skippers, which has proved highly satisfactory. But with the time approaching for replacement, Andrew Bryce went to Optare with a very clear idea of what he wanted. Seating capacity had to be increased to 30, he wanted a low floor but no intrusion of wheel-arches to restrict seating. This meant the wheels had to be as near the four corners of the bus as possible. There was no reason just because the bus was less than full-sized that the destination indicators should be miniature too and, as Andrew Bryce succinctly put it, people don't get any thinner just because they are sitting in a small bus, so it had to be as wide as a big one.

Optare was at first somewhat reluctant to go the whole way but Wilts & Dorset is a valued customer and got exactly what it wanted: the Solo. Ironically, it has proved so popular with other operators that Optare now has more Solo orders than it ever thought possible. The Solos and

24

the Spectras, bearing the slogan 'Salisbury's future is riding on it', have proved a great success. But wouldn't it be nice if the Government, which initially set so much store by its commitment to public transport, could match Wilts & Dorset's enterprise?

Solos have also appeared in Poole and work a number of services in and around the town, to Bournemouth, and beyond. In all, the company ordered 85, all of which should be in service before 1999 is out.

The backbone of the double-deck fleet is Optare's Spectra, based on DAF DB250 chassis. Ten arrived in 1993 and, prior to the low-floor examples, a fleet of 47 was built up — the largest in the country. The Spectra is a most handsome bus and a delight to ride in. At times I travel home from work in one, having the upper deck entirely to myself as we bowl along the picturesque A351 from Swanage. You might ask how it can be economic to run a double-decker when a small single-decker would suffice, but Wilts & Dorset is careful to work out just when and where a double-decker is appropriate over a whole day's schedule, bearing in mind school journeys, rush hours, etc.

Interesting additions to the fleet early in 1998 were 11 DAFs, new to Walls of Manchester two years earlier, which, following the Stagecoach takeover of that company's operations, were put up for sale. Six are Northern Counties-bodied double-deckers; the remaining five are Ikarus-bodied single-deckers. All except one of the single-deckers are based at Poole, the exception being sent on to the subsidiary fleet of Damory Coaches of Blandford. The only other full-size single-deckers in the

Wilts & Dorset fleet are six Optare-bodied DAF SB220 48-seat Deltas delivered in 1993.

Schools contracts provide much business for the company. I asked Andrew Bryce about that perennial bane of such operations, bad behaviour. 'Some schools take the attitude that responsibility for their pupils ends the moment they leave the premises; others are mindful of their reputation and make it clear that any bad behaviour reflects on this and is not tolerated.'

He went on to say that with parents becoming ever more aware of choice they are shopping around much more, often sending their offspring to schools some distance from home — all good business for Wilts & Dorset. 'At one time County Hall handled all the arrangements with bus companies. Now this responsibility has in some cases passed to schools and colleges. We know that often they have neither the time nor expertise to deal with it so we offer a complete package — not merely providing the bus, but planning routes, providing tickets and close monitoring of operations in their early days.'

Vandalism is not much of a problem in Wilts & Dorset territory, although there is one notorious estate in the Poole area where crews faced real danger on late evening runs in the late 1980s, particularly on Fridays and Saturdays. 'It was all very well for us to sit here and say you must keep going for the sake of all the responsible residents to whom the bus service is a real lifeline, but if drivers were being abused, seat cushions were being hurled out of the windows and so forth,

you had great sympathy with the drivers who feared for their safety.

'It was remarkable that when we substituted a small single-decker, with another as relief if necessary, for a double-decker, problems inside the vehicles virtually vanished. If there are only 23 of you and you are sitting very close to the driver then you think twice before

Below:
There's a long tradition of open-top operation in the Bournemouth area, as illustrated by a Bristol K bound for Swanage. The full-front conversion was carried out by Hants & Dorset.

Bottom:
Bristol LHs were phased out of the Wilts & Dorset fleet during 1999. This 1980 bus, photographed in Swanage in April 1998, was one of the last.

misbehaving. The chief problems now are young children who throw stones as the bus enters the estate. It then does a circular run and the poor driver knows he has to face them again as he drives out. The children are too young to be prosecuted and simply run away. But on the whole our problems are very minor compared to other companies. Even Yellow Bus has suffered incidents on weekend evenings in Bournemouth where drunks have been known to break upstairs windows and climb on the roof whilst the bus is driving along.'

However, riding a Wilts & Dorset bus is generally a pleasurable experience, whether deep into the Dorset, Wiltshire or Hampshire countryside or beside the sea in Bournemouth, Poole or elsewhere along the coast. Wilts & Dorset covers much of the New Forest and as far east as Southampton, as far north as Swindon and westwards

preserved ECW-bodied Bristol K or L, I think what a beautifully proportioned bus it is, and I have developed a sudden affection for Nationals and VRs now that they are elderly and fast becoming endangered species.

Wilts and Dorset's Nationals, never a significant part of the fleet, have now gone — 'We weren't sorry to see the back of them,' says Andrew Bryce — but there are still 36 VRs, 28 of which are being extensively refurbished so that internally they are rather like the Spectras. Andrew Bryce sees them as still having a future with the company. They are needed for school runs and during peak periods.

Because NBC failed to invest in new double-deckers in the first half of the 1980s, there is a dearth of elderly but still serviceable vehicles on the second-hand market and therefore it made sense to implement a major internal

to Bath. The last-named is served by the X4, a route worked jointly with Badgerline, a relationship which survived even during the days when they were trying to put Wilts & Dorset out of business in 1987 by running buses on just about every route in Salisbury.

More competition came from Badgerline's partner, Southern Vectis, in Bournemouth and Poole. In the event, both interlopers retired with bloody noses, Badgerline losing almost £1 million, which was what the management had paid to buy the company from NBC a little earlier. The new management of Wilts & Dorset emerged from this bruising experience determined to make a success of what had not until then been a particularly profitable segment of NBC, and this they certainly have done.

The precursors of the present company had by the 1960s both taken on the appearance of typical Tilling concerns, running a pretty dull selection of standard Bristol/ECW products. Now I've probably upset thousands of discerning readers, but to one whose infant loyalties were divided between London Transport, Southdown and Midland Red, you may just appreciate my point of view. However, there is very little logic in bus enthusiasts' addictions. Especially as every time I come across a

Top:
A fine line-up at Poole depot in 1978.

Above:
In NBC days Hants & Dorset served Salisbury. A Leyland National in unrelieved poppy red loads in the city centre.

upgrading on the VRs — mechanically still very sound — by getting rid of leaks and rattling windows and making all-round improvements.

Andrew Bryce was not sorry to see the last of the Nationals but, the RE, like the VR, gave the company excellent service and 'looked as if it could go on for ever'. It would be hard for the most besotted addict to claim that the VR's predecessor, the Lodekka — with its bulging, humped front, some with gaping holes between decks to let the air in, oversized wheels and generally peculiar lines — was a pretty bus, although it certainly had character. The final version, the FLF, could look very impressive when newly turned out in poppy red.

The ECW-bodied LS and early MW were among the best-looking coaches of their generation, with remarkably clean lines, while the later REs were also handsome vehicles. The principal coach operator in the Poole and Bournemouth area for generations was Royal Blue. Between 1935 and 1937 Hants & Dorset worked Royal Blue excursions and tours, and as partners in the Tilling Group an agreement ensured that Royal Blue worked express services between Bournemouth and London and along the South Coast, Bournemouth being the vehicle operating centre.

Today's Wilts & Dorset coach fleet consists of three Bova Futuras used on National Express work, two Plaxton-bodied DAFs for the X4 and seven Duple Laser-bodied Leyland Tigers. All the coaches are based in Salisbury.

Like most Tilling companies in the immediate postwar years, Hants & Dorset bought a number of non-standard vehicles, pleased to lay its hands on any sort of new bus and thus six AEC Regent IIIs with Northern Counties lowbridge bodywork were delivered in 1949 and worked out of Bournemouth for many years. My original stay in Hants & Dorset territory ended shortly after VE Day,

1945. The buses I knew best and travelled on regularly were ECW-bodied Ks and similar-looking Brush-bodied Leyland TD4 and TD5 Titans, rather handsome and typically late 1930s.

At the age of seven I can't recall noticing the difference between Bristol and Leyland radiators — yes, I know I should have done — but there was no mistaking the Leyland sound. Earlier in the war, in 1940, we had been evacuated to Sussex, which meant Southdown. Even at the tender age of two and some months I had instantly fallen for the throaty roar of Southdown's oil-engined Titans and Tigers, so different from the aspirated gasp of the petrol-engined STs or the genteel purr of the STLs which passed our road back home in Thornton Heath.

I think most of the Bournemouth to Poole services — there were four, numbered logically enough 1 to 4 — were worked by Bristols for I can recall hearing one morning from our flat in St Michael's Road the roar of a Leyland engine climbing Poole Hill and wondering if this meant Southdown had taken over the route. So Leylands must have been relatively rare. There were also some austere-looking utility buses, one of which was painted grey all over and worked the local service from Poole to Upton. Nine Guy Arabs and 11 Bristol Ks composed Hants & Dorset's wartime acquisitions so presumably it was one of these — probably a Bristol, as the different note produced by a Guy Arab would surely have struck me.

One could hardly escape the war wherever one went in Bournemouth in 1944-5. Coming from the London

Below:
Royal Blue served the Bournemouth area — although in 1979 the name appeared somewhat inappropriate on an all-white livery. An ECW-bodied Bristol RE loads in Poole for Westward Ho!, one of the few place names to feature an exclamation mark.

suburbs we were pretty scornful of our landlord's oft-repeated assertion that 'Jerry will have another go at Bournemouth before the war's over,' but he had some justification for on 23 May 1943 the Luftwaffe had wreaked considerable damage. Hants & Dorset had the windows blown out of 25 buses standing in the open in the bus station, although, fortunately, all the passengers and crews had taken cover and were unhurt. Shortly before our arrival Allied troops had landed in Normandy, a mere 30min across the Channel by troop-carrying Dakota — on a clear night it was possible to see flashes in the sky above the Cherbourg peninsula from St Aldhelm's Head, west of Swanage.

Bournemouth was awash with Americans, the first I'd ever seen apart from on the cinema screen. Looking back more than 50 years I can see they must have been very young, many not yet out of their teens. One, as I came out of church with my parents on Christmas Day, handed me a bar of chocolate, which was deliciously different from any I'd tasted before. On another occasion on the upper deck of a Number 3 near County Gates I overheard one say to another that he felt nostalgic for home and I had to ask my mother what the word meant.

VE Day came, our house was repaired, more or less, we returned and it would be almost 30 years before I travelled on a Hants & Dorset bus again.

Coming back to Dorset in 1977 and finding a fleet of red buses took some getting used to, although green reappeared for a few years in 1979 when six-year-old VRs were bought from Southern Vectis and retained their original livery until due for overhaul. At that time the

Daimler Fleetline featured quite significantly, with six Roe-bodied examples bought new in 1971 and a further 10 DMSs which came from London Transport in 1976-7. Having moved from the London area, the last sight I expected to see passing our front door was this familiar shape. I had rather a soft spot for the much-maligned DMS, and so it seems did Wilts & Dorset, for it got something like 10 years' service out of its examples.

With the demise of Bristol and the end of VR production Wilts & Dorset turned to its successor, the Leyland Olympian. It bought five ECW-bodied new ones in 1984, with coach-type seats and painted in dual-purpose livery. However, the majority of Olympians were second-hand. Two arrived from North Devon in 1986 and five more from the West Yorkshire PTE the following year, all with convertible open tops and cutaway front panelling for use on the Sandbanks Ferry and the 150 Bournemouth to Swanage service. A Roe-bodied Olympian was bought from Metrobus in 1982, six more Roe-bodied examples came from County Bus in 1990, three ECW-bodied ones from Crosville Wales the same year, another Roe-bodied one from Stevensons in 1991, and three East Lancs-bodied ones, also from Stevensons, in 1990.

It has to be said that many of the Olympians are approaching, if they have not already reached, their sell-by date. Some have been withdrawn, and the refurbished VRs will certainly outlast them. Which brings us round full circle to the present day.

Wilts & Dorset operates one of the most interesting and up-to-date fleets in the country. There is no cross-

Right:
Wilts & Dorset ran ex-London Fleetlines, in rather more rural surroundings than they were originally operated.

Right:
In the face of post-deregulation competition Wilts & Dorset bought some Bristol VRs from West Midlands. Two flank a standard ECW-bodied bus in Poole garage in 1987.

subsidy, so each service has to be self-supporting; hence the variety of vehicles ranging from 23-seaters to full-size double-deckers.

Rather like Bournemouth-based Yellow Buses, covered in *Buses Yearbook 1999*, there is much seasonal variation, something I particularly notice on our local 142/3/4 Swanage to Poole routes. Between October and April I can usually command the front seat upstairs. This gives me a wonderful view of the countryside compared with that low down from my Datsun, especially on the top road between Langton Matravers and Kingston, with the sea on three sides and the romantic ruins of Corfe Castle

and the distant high rise flats and offices of Poole and Bournemouth across Poole Harbour on the fourth. But once the grockles (Dorset for visitors) come out from their winter hibernation it is a different matter.

So if you are bored with corporate liveries and corporate buses, come to Dorset and see what real individuality means.

I'd like to thank Andrew Bryce for his help with the preparation and checking of this article, although clearly the opinions and any inaccuracies are mine alone.

Right:
New and second-hand Olympians are operated — but may be outlived by refurbished VRTs. This ECW-bodied bus is used in a joint operation with Guide Friday. It is seen at Salisbury station in the summer of 1998.

Below:
Much of Wilts & Dorset's territory is rural. An ex-Southern National Bristol RE illustrates the point on the route between Kingston and Corfe Castle.

Tellygraphic Memory

A Northern General Atlantean sweeps past James Bolam on the opening credits for *Whatever Happened to the Likely Lads?*

Hero of the Industry

Geoffrey Hilditch was perhaps better known to enthusiasts by his pen-name, Gortonian, but in the industry he was driving for technical innovation. He supported the Maxwell gearbox, the Dennis Dominator and Falcon H, and was awarded an OBE before joining the Department of Transport as a consultant in the run-up to deregulation.

The Flashing Blade

Every generation needs a mythical hero, who has the ability to overcome any opponent with legendary power and skill. All the better if these powers cannot be tested in the real world — the myth can only be damaged by sordid reality. And so it was with cunning and restraint that BLMC displayed the V8-engined AEC Sabre in 1970 to whet everyone's appetite before announcing that it would never enter production. The reality was that with Bedford and Ford featherweights dominating the coach scene and REMHs covering the toughest duties, no market existed for the complex and expensive Sabre. But BLMC gained kudos for its ingenuity.

Are You Being Served?

This was not the attitude bus buyers encountered during the bus shortages of the early and mid-1970s — BLMC's aggressive stance with the National came down to Like It Or Lump It. Of course, BL knew that standardisation and elimination of short-run variants would pay off. But operators didn't see it that way until hit by the stern reality of deregulation since which major success has come to those chassis and body manufacturers who keep focused on unit cost. Sadly it was rather too late to help Workington.

The Persuaders

Exotic strangers with sophisticated tendencies, adventuring in a strange land — Scotland. Yes, Volvo had freewheeled into town with those attention-getting steeds, the thoroughbred B58 and the continental B59. Coach operator Douglas Park of Hamilton was one of the first to be persuaded that the B58 was the answer, but with the B59 no one knew what the question was. The Scottish Bus Group was going to need a lot of persuading to accept these mysterious foreign things but in the end the Persuaders won through and it was SBG, not Volvo, which hit the large stack of empty cardboard boxes.

Dad's Army

The Bedford SB was an old soldier, bought not just as a coach with Duple or Plaxton bodywork (although lots were still bought), but for a long time SB5 buses were thought to be the only vehicles suitable for rural roads. Navy blue ones soldiered around the Western Isles and less remote places like Llangollen. Ultimately, the need for 40-seat coaches (once a large sector of the market, also covered by the PSU4 Leopard) vanished as parties of potential coach hirers thoughtfully rounded themselves up and down into units of 25 or 50, suitable for minis or full-size vehicles. I don't pretend to understand how it happened but it certainly killed off the midi-sized coach. Just one of those mysteries.

Rock Follies

Let's take a classic idea like a rock band or a Fleetline, add a spicy twist or two to the usual ingredients, bring in a big name and make a soap opera out of it. There will be laughter, tears, success and a lot of shouting. At the end of the day, one or two have had their fingers burnt but no one has been seriously short-changed and child prodigy Hesta can go on to bigger and better things.

The Sweeney

Cor, what a blag! This Ailsa goes like a dream and there's three-abreast seat upstairs where you can get cosy with your bird. The turbocharged engine's a bit of alright as well guv. Let's just hope none of the villains start using these for their getaways, eh?

Last of the Summer Wine

Guy Arab and his mates Regent and Titan pottered up and down the hills of Yorkshire throughout the 1970s but the time for their gentle potterings had passed and they were swept aside by more modern fare as the decade closed. Age has withered and custom staled their infinite variety.

GLE EYED 2: 1970s

Corporate Image Is In

1970s vehicles are much more complex than previously with turbochargers, encapsulated engines and kneeling Nationals in vogue

Above:

ROCK FOLLIES

A transformed Fleetline? The Dominator took over when the Fleetline dropped out of the scene. Leicester built up a large fleet with East Lancs bodies.

Left:

LAST OF THE SUMMER WINE

Green Bus Service stuck with good old-fashioned buses. A Massey-bodied Titan meets an East Lancs-bodied Tiger Cub in Armitage in 1988.

BOOMING
DEMAND
for Secondhand Buses

In the years immediately after local bus deregulation there was a healthy market in good used buses. Alan Millar explores.

TITAN
No. 1

MULTI-RIDE

A New Leyland Titan for London Transport

THX 401S

TITAN
No. 2

MULTI-RIDE

A New Leyland Titan for London Transport

THX 402S

TITAN
No. 3

Secondhand buses became respectable in the late 1980s. As all the rule books which governed their past lives were torn up, operators found themselves selling buses they would otherwise have kept for years to come, while others accepted that they no longer needed brand-new vehicles every time they chose to upgrade their fleets.

In the jargon of the age, we're talking of 'late model' or 'mid-life' vehicles. If they were cars, and especially if they were American ones being sold on their native heath, we'd call them 'pre-owned' or, better still, 'pre-enjoyed' vehicles and they'd change hands for substantial sums of money. They're not the old bangers or late-life vehicles which have always kept a sector of the bus industry in business.

For decades, major operators worked on replacement cycles of around 15 years. This wasn't necessarily because they were thinking that far ahead, but they could be reasonably confident that a bus bought new, say, in 1955 would still have a role to play until it was replaced by a bigger bus in 1970. They could be equally sure that the replacement would be good for the next 15 years. Indeed, they would far more often mould their services around the buses they operated, than change their fleets to suit new services.

Fifteen-year cycles turned buses into assets to be written down to a nominal value over a lengthy period. When they were finally sold — either to breakers or dealers — their original owners didn't expect to raise much cash from their disposal. But the best few survivors

— often from fleets like Ribble, Trent or Southdown — spared many independents from even thinking about buying new vehicles.

Most bigger fleets considered secondhand purchases only in exceptional circumstances when, for some reason

Opposite:
When the first three Leyland Titans for London Transport were paraded round a remarkably traffic-free Parliament Square in 1978 there was no thought that such a complex bus would find ready buyers on the second-hand market little over a decade later. Leyland

Opposite above:
As London's new Titans arrived, the unloved Swifts and Merlins were departing. Few found further service outside London. Despite efforts by LT to find overseas buyers, most were sold for scrap. One — still less than 10 years old — is towed up the A1 to a breaker's yard in Yorkshire. SJB

Below:
The acquisition by Maidstone & District of Dennis Dominators from East Staffordshire District Council actually pre-dated deregulation and happened while M&D was still part of the National Bus Company. When acquired by M&D the buses were around six years old, at a time when such relatively young double-deckers were rarely available on the second-hand market. This is a post-privatisation view, and while still in NBC green, the old double-N logo alongside the fleetname has been neatly replaced by a new M&D symbol. SJB

or other, they were desperately short of serviceable rolling stock. And if they were part of one of the bigger groups, those fleets' needs could usually be met by transferring surplus vehicles from another group company.

There were exceptions to this pattern. Manufacturers' demonstrators, often highly specified and exceptionally well cared for, made an acceptable substitute for new vehicles, but there weren't many of them.

And occasionally some quite extraordinary circumstances unleashed nearly-new buses on the market. On a small scale, the Tilling Group had no long-term use for the four lowbridge Leyland Atlanteans it acquired with Silver Star of Porton Down in the 1960s. A much more widely-shared bargain came in the mid to late 1950s when London Transport discovered it had over-ordered RTs and RTLs and began selling these highly desirable machines in quantities that appealed not only to independents but also to the municipal fleets in Walsall, Bradford and Dundee.

History repeated itself 20 years later when London's DMS Fleetlines were sold prematurely and passenger transport executives, municipals and big group companies spotted a bargain at a time when the new bus

grant scheme's demise began to inflate new vehicle prices. But the mid-life buses had to match operators' needs. Few fleets wanted the late 1960s rear-engined single-deckers which London Transport and other fleets sold off well before their 10th birthdays.

The whole pattern of supply and demand changed with the two big deregulation moves initiated by the Conservatives in 1984 and 1985. First, London Transport's monopoly of the capital's bus market was broken, opening up the network to competitive tendering, with operators bidding for contracts to run routes for periods of up to five years, price being a critical factor. Fifteen-year cycles became irrelevant.

Then the 1985 Transport Act paved the way for the massive changes made in the rest of the country, opening routes up to competition, breaking up the bigger groups initially into independent businesses, and ending the massive fares subsidies in places like South Yorkshire where cheap travel had begun to reverse decades of declining use of bus services. It was even less easy for operators outside London to predict what would happen over the next 15 days, let alone 15 years, and they were waking up fast to a whole new set of rapidly changing commercial circumstances.

As deregulation loomed in October 1986, many fleets concluded that they had far too many buses for their future needs. They also realised that they needed fewer big buses and many more little ones. With the break-up of the bigger groups, beginning with the National Bus Company, surplus buses could no longer simply be switched from one part of the country to another for a nominal sum or in exchange for a different type of bus of similar value. They would have to change hands for real money at prices that reflected their market value.

Demand for these buses would come from three main sectors: smaller operators providing new competition for the established order; fleets winning tenders in London and elsewhere; and bigger fleets looking for attractively-priced newer vehicles they could no longer obtain by inter-fleet transfers.

The process began as the passenger transport executives transferred their buses to arm's length passenger transport companies and many of them adjusted to the dual realities of losing big subsidies and becoming exposed to rapidly increasing competition. To an extent, they could just accelerate the withdrawal of their oldest buses and clear out non-standard types like the last Bristol VRTs in Merseyside and the West Midlands. But the cuts were so deep that some highly attractive buses came on to the secondhand market.

It's hard to say now if these buses sold because new operators were keen to establish competitive services, or if the competitive services started because there were good secondhand buses on the market. But the buses were available and lots of people bought them.

The biggest single source was Greater Manchester Transport which identified around 600 vehicles it wanted to sell in the immediate aftermath of deregulation and the creation of Greater Manchester Buses. Around 450 were rendered surplus by 1986 route cuts and increased operating efficiencies; others were replaced later by minibuses as GM Buses faced competition from BET's short-lived Bee Line Buzz operation in Stockport and south Manchester.

To shift them, it set up a joint venture company with coach dealer Kirkby Central — which later took over Plaxton. Most of the buses were early 1970s Atlanteans and Fleetlines, but there also were nine and 10-year-old

Fleetlines and Nationals and five to eight-year-old oddities like 15 of the very few Leyland Titans built for service outside London, 10 MCW Metrobuses with hydraulic brakes and a quartet of early Dennis Dominators.

The Manchester buses expanded a market first tapped by the London DMSs and for prices of between £5,000 and £22,000 they found such hitherto unexpected new homes in municipal fleets, former NBC and Scottish Bus Group companies and — most extraordinary of all — Yorkshire Rider, the former West Yorkshire PTE fleet which snapped up 76 Atlanteans and Fleetlines.

Yorkshire Rider's purchase showed how quickly the industry had upset itself into a topsy-turvy world of changing priorities and short-term objectives. For it had not long since declined to take on the PTE's commitments to lease 42 significantly newer Leyland Olympians and 10 Metrobuses. Faced with this unique opportunity to escape from a financially unattractive arrangement, it seems that Rider gambled on being able to buy the buses direct from the leasing company, but if that was the plan it backfired.

Below:
Municipally-owned fleets also provided new homes for unwanted Greater Manchester buses. This Northern Counties-bodied Atlantean was bought by Hyndburn Transport. SJB

In a market where few operators were buying new double-deckers, Rider was outbid in the auction. Blackpool Transport took three Olympians as replacements for buses lost in a fire, and most of the other 49 went to Ensignbus, the Essex dealer which had made a small fortune out of selling on most of the London DMSs.

Fate could hardly have delivered a better bunch of buses on to the secondhand market in 1986/7. Chester, which was enlarging and updating its council-owned fleet with the aid of some astute purchases of secondhand Olympians and Dennis Dominators, took two of the Olympians. Eleven more went to ex-NBC fleets Cambus, Cheltenham & Gloucester, Wilts & Dorset and Southern National, and six were exported to Citybus in Hong Kong. Metrobus of Orpington took 11 for London Transport-tendered routes, while provincial independents A1 of Ardrossan, Stevenson's of Uttoxeter and Turner of Brown Edge (soon taken over by ex-NBC company PMT) shared the other nine.

Most of the Metrobuses went either to Stevenson's or to a secondhand buyer no one would ever have dreamed of a year or two earlier. London Buses, the arm's length

inheritor of London Transport's bus fleet, took four (and five of the Manchester Metrobuses) as it began to adjust itself to a world of open competition. Even more amazingly, it bought some mid-1970s Ailsa double-deckers from the West Midlands and South Yorkshire PTE fleets, along with some new buses that, ironically, would make their own quick way on to the secondhand market.

The Ailsas and some reacquired DMS Fleetlines formed part of the specially liveried fleets amassed to run tendered route contracts in northwest and southeast London — the red/cream Harrow Buses and blue/cream Bexleybus networks. To go with them, 55 new double-deckers were leased from Roadlease, the Kirkby/Plaxton finance division. There were 27 Mark II Metrobuses for Harrow and 28 Manchester-specification Olympians with Northern Counties bodies for Bexleybus; none conformed in any significant way to what people had come to regard as London's specifications.

The subsequent fate of the only London Buses 'deckers supplied between the last big batch of Olympians and the first trickle of new deliveries in 1989 owes everything to the then Government's treatment of nationalised industries like London Buses.

The three-year Harrow and Bexley contracts demanded a proportion of new buses. Private operators bidding for these same routes could have leased new buses for a longer period on the assumption that they could either find other work or other buyers for them if the route contracts were lost after three years. Treasury rules limited the risks London Buses could take, compelling it to take out three-year leases, even though that was a more expensive option.

Sod's Law did its worst in 1990 when the routes were retendered. Metroline, the new London Buses subsidiary running Harrow Buses, and Selkent, running Bexleybus, lost most of the contracts and all 55 buses went back to Roadlease. Most of the Olympians went to Busways' former Tyne & Wear PTE fleet and around half the Metrobuses went to council-owned Reading Buses. One Olympian was exported to the Far East island of Sentosa, while other buyers for the two types were Fareway of Liverpool, Great Yarmouth Transport, Capital Citybus, Finglands of Manchester and Longstaff of Mirfield — another mix of expanding urban independents, a traditional independent and a small municipal.

By then, Ensign was selling older but still comparatively modern Metrobuses rendered surplus to requirements in South Yorkshire, and the AJS Group was sorting out its inheritance of ex-London Country Olympians. Some were reallocated within the short-lived group's empire, moving from loss-making routes in Hertfordshire and Essex to Keighley & District in profitable West Yorkshire, but the value of others was realised by selling them on the open market to Wilts & Dorset. The small numbers of Olympians then operated by the municipal fleets in Southampton, Plymouth and Nottingham also found new owners.

The fate of some of the Scottish Bus Group's newer buses reflected some of its subsidiaries' traumas as they headed for privatisation in 1990/1. Deprived of an internal market for mid-life buses, it let go of vehicles it would have simply reallocated a few years before.

The most dramatic effects were at Kelvin, the new subsidiary formed in 1985 to run an expanded network of routes to the north of Glasgow. It came off worse in a duel with Strathclyde Buses, clocking up losses of around £3 million and earning a stiff rebuke from the traffic commissioner for what he called its 'deplorable' standards of maintenance. A series of fleet cuts began in August 1987 and continued after Central Scottish and Kelvin were merged in 1989 to create Kelvin Central, clearing well over 200 buses in the process.

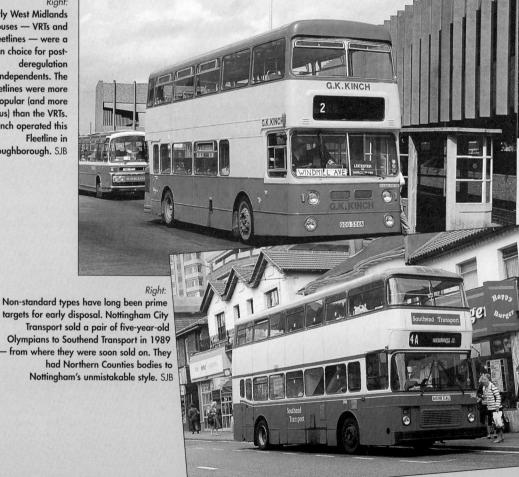

Right:
Elderly West Midlands buses — VRTs and Fleetlines — were a common choice for post-deregulation independents. The Fleetlines were more popular (and more numerous) than the VRTs. Kinch operated this Fleetline in Loughborough. SJB

Right:
Non-standard types have long been prime targets for early disposal. Nottingham City Transport sold a pair of five-year-old Olympians to Southend Transport in 1989 — from where they were soon sold on. They had Northern Counties bodies to Nottingham's unmistakable style. SJB

Some found homes elsewhere in SBG, but the secondhand market benefited first from the appearance of dozens of standard SBG Leyland Leopards with Alexander Y-type bodies, followed speedily by Leyland Nationals, a handful of lowheight Alexander-bodied Metrobuses and some Seddon Pennine 7s. Most of the Leopards went to independents, but council-owned Blackburn got four and Stagecoach — in the early stages of its nationwide expansion — took others along with a few Nationals. Other Nationals went to SUT and West Riding, while Stevensons took several Seddons along with what had been SBG's only Leyland Lynx.

Ensign bought Metrobuses, keeping three for its own bus fleet which was subsequently sold to become Capital Citybus. North Western and Midland Red North, ex-NBC companies by then owned by the Drawlane group, bought some of the others to help make up for their owner's very low investment in new buses; other Kelvin Central Metrobus buyers included Manchester independents Bullock of Cheadle and Stuart of Hyde.

Kelvin's problems had led to six rare new Leyland Lion double-deckers being diverted to fellow SBG subsidiary Clydeside in 1987. By 1993/4, Clydeside was owned by its employees and was selling most of its modern double-deckers in quest of a better trading performance. Five of the Lions went to Chester for park-&-ride work, the sixth to Gloucestershire independent Cotterell of Mitcheldean, while some slightly older Dominators were shipped to Hong Kong and older secondhand Leopards took their place.

A couple of years earlier, just after Highland Scottish was sold, it abandoned its busiest routes around Inverness in the face of competition from Stagecoach and sold its newest vehicles. Of its two dozen Olympians, 13 went to Stagecoach Ribble along with seven older Leopards, while the others went to Liverbus, Chester and Capital Citybus — by now familiar names if you're identifying a pattern to this story.

For quite different reasons, Harry Blundred's Transit Holdings sold big quantities of mid-life double-deckers in the late 1980s as it converted its Devon General and South Midland services to higher frequency minibus operation. Here again, there was nowhere to cascade these vehicles which were highly attractive to other buyers. Stagecoach, Western Travel, Midland Fox and Solent Blueline eagerly acquired what mostly were Bristol VRTs; but Western Travel's haul included six ex-Manchester Titans rendered surplus to requirements for the second time in their then short lives.

There have been many other sales of similarly modern rolling stock, like ex-Crosville Olympians bought by Happy Al's of Birkenhead after Crosville changed hands in 1989, and batches of well-maintained Trent Olympians more recently bought by Blackpool and Ipswich's municipal fleets. Thirty nearly new West Midlands Sherpa minibuses were sold to Yorkshire Rider in 1987 and Strathclyde Buses bought batches of MCW Metrorider minibuses from Colchester, Southampton, Dublin Bus and The Eden of West Auckland.

Left:
One of the great surprises of deregulation was the demand from operators around the country for London Buses' Routemasters. They were particularly popular in Scotland. Strathtay Scottish was one of three Scottish Bus Group subsidiaries to buy RMs, operating them in Perth and, as seen here, Dundee. SJB

Top:

The Leyland National, never popular with small operators when it was new, has been the mainstay of many smaller fleets in the 15 years since deregulation. Lanarkshire operator McKindless was running this pair of ex-Ribble vehicles in 1990 — both in as-acquired condition. The bus on the left carries the familiar colours of a rather larger Scottish operator; that on the right is in Ribble's final pre-Stagecoach livery of NBC red with grey and white relief. SJB

Above:

London was the only significant user of Titans, and the late 1980s saw them being bought by a disparate collection of fleets large and small. Merseyside Transport was the biggest user and many of those it acquired ran for some considerable time in London red. Tower Hill is a particularly apt destination. SJB

Above right:

While London was busy selling Routemasters it was also buying an odd assortment of pre-owned Ailsas and Metrobuses. This Mark II Metrobus was originally operated by the West Yorkshire PTE and is seen in service with London Northern at Potters Bar in 1990. SJB

Now that the industry has settled down into a more stable state with new groups owning the major fleets, open market sales of mid-life buses are becoming less common and inter-group transfers are shuttling buses up and down the country once again. But the secondhand market is unlikely to die.

London Transport's tendering regime will cascade mid-life buses out of the capital by one means or another. Even in the late 1990s, FirstGroup and Arriva were both buying secondhand Dennis Falcons for two of their fleets. And the industry's adoption of other forms of vehicle acquisition is helping maintain a steady flow of modern secondhand buses.

The Harrow and Bexley experiences may have been far from perfect, but leasing and rental has become much more common, with businesses like Dawsonrentals, Mistral (formerly Cheshire Bus and Coach) and Arriva Bus and Coach (formerly Hughes DAF) emerging as major players, supplying new and nearly new buses to

fleets which a few years ago would have made do with the likes of Greater Manchester's 1986 cast-offs. They also provide many of the buses used at major airports and keep their fleets up-to-date by regularly selling their older buses on the secondhand market.

This is all part of a process which has seen the industry change dramatically to regard its buses as assets which have a resale value at any stage in their lives, and a value which can be realised by selling them when it makes most financial sense. Stagecoach has demonstrated this change by selling modern, standard specification buses along with routes and garages when there have been strategic reasons for it to dispose of parts of its businesses.

So relatively modern Olympians went when its Huntingdon garage was sold to Julian Peddle's MK Metro in 1997 (and subsequently sold on to Blazefield Holdings), nearly new Volvo B10Ms went to the EYMS Group when the original Stagecoach Manchester

operation was sold in 1995, and similarly modern B10Ms and Dennis Darts went in separate sales of businesses in Glasgow. Before 1985, you would more likely expect a company to offload its oldest buses in such a deal, if indeed any vehicles were involved.

The process could change further if a recent kite-flying Stagecoach exercise is ever revived for real. For on 28 August 1997, many bus managers were taken aback as they read their 52-page copy of the trade magazine *Coach & Bus Week*. It's one of the two main advertising mediums for secondhand buses and, as they flicked their way past news of Travel West Midlands' initial order for 100 lowfloor Mercedes-Benz O405Ns and the customary glossy advertisements for new buses and coaches, the managers' journey to the small ads for secondhand vehicles at the back of the magazine was halted by a full-page glossy colour ad on page 15 for some far-from-old and potentially highly attractive vehicles.

Stagecoach was testing the market for 12-year-old Alexander-bodied Olympians in the Busways fleet and for the first of its large batches of Volvo B10M single-deckers, Cumberland machines then not yet five years old. Potential buyers were invited to contact the group's technical engineer with a view to taking things further.

Little more happened. But I gather at least one of the smaller groups with a recent history of investing in new and modern secondhand vehicles was interested in the Olympians and I'd be amazed if others didn't look at them, too, along with the B10Ms.

The inside story is that, as a company founded and developed by a particularly astute accountant, Stagecoach was eager to find out how the figures would add up if it replaced its buses far more frequently and long before it needed to spend big sums of money refurbishing them in mid-life. Maybe the sums didn't add up attractively in 1997, but there's a fair chance that they might at some time in the future and, if they do, you can expect a whole new market in modern secondhand buses to be opened up.

Fifteen-year replacement cycles would finally be consigned to distant history. So might 15-year operating lives.

Above:
Stagecoach has Titans in a variety of locations, most displaced from its London fleets. More unusual is this former West Midlands bus, seen in Gloucester operating for Red & White. SJB

Right:
London's Fleetlines, sold off prematurely from the end of the 1980s, were snapped up by operators around the country, from Highland Omnibuses in the north to Western National in the south. Midland Red (South) ran this late example. The location is Stratford-upon-Avon. SJB

DOUBLE DECKERS
at the Cross-roads

Double-deck bus design is undergoing its most radical change for 40 years with the arrival of new low-floor models. Stewart J. Brown looks at the implications. Is it the end of the road for the double-decker...?

O ne of the less well publicised features of the new millennium is the change which is taking place in double-deck bus design. As I write this, at the start of 1999, some of the last of what might be described as old-style double-deckers are being built by Alexander and Northern Counties — R-types, Royales and Palatines. Production of East Lancs Cityzens is about to cease and the last of the original Optare Spectras was built in 1998.

In their place are coming a new generation of low-floor double-deckers with step-free entrances — Alexander's ALX400, Northern Counties' President (marketed under the Plaxton name), East Lancs' Lolyne and Optare's low-floor Spectra.

By the time this appears in print the last two-step double-deckers for UK service should have been delivered — and with them a whole range of established chassis will be consigned to history: the Volvo Olympian and Citybus, Dennis Arrow, Scania N113 and the original DAF DB250.

Now, cynics and those with long memories are quick to point out that the low-floor double-decker, being proclaimed as an invention of the 1990s, has a long and honourable history. Setting aside the pioneering — and unsuccessful — effort by Gilford at the start of the 1930s, buses with single-step entrances were in volume production 40 years ago.

Below:
'Tomorrow's standards today' proclaims the lettering on this Leyland B15 prototype. The two-step entrance is clearly visible, yet Leyland had done considerable research into the mobility of elderly people and claimed that the Titan — as the B15 became — would open up bus travel to an extra two million people. AEC

Most early Leyland Atlanteans, for example, had a step-free platform, with a flat floor extending back to the area just ahead of the rear axle where there was a step up to the rear seating area. The rival Fleetline from Daimler was similar in layout, and with its drop-centre rear axle could provide a step-free ramped gangway right to the rear of the lower saloon.

Front-engined models like the Bristol Lodekka and Dennis Loline were likewise able to offer step-free access to the lower deck, although in these and other similar designs the aim was not to eliminate steps, but to reduce overall vehicle height.

Back in the 1960s bus operators were not overly concerned about access for disabled passengers — and the idea of wheeling a baby buggy onto a bus was unimaginable, no doubt in part because many babies were still being wheeled around in ungainly Silver Cross prams.

To eliminate the step in the gangway towards the rear of the lower deck of the Atlantean, a number of fleets — Liverpool Corporation was a pioneer here — opted for a two-step entrance and a ramped, step-free, gangway. This was designed to reduce the risk of passengers tripping over the step midway down the saloon.

The merits of two-step entrances were debated for the rest of the 1960s, but by the early 1970s most operators accepted that a two-step entrance and gently ramped gangway was the best option. A few — most notably Bournemouth Corporation — stuck with a single-step entrance, but for most big fleets the two-step layout was preferred. Some were shallow steps — as on National Bus Company ECW-bodied Bristol VRTs. Others were relatively deep steps, as on London Transport's DMS-class Fleetlines.

Above:

Southdown bought one batch of Volvo Citybuses with particularly tall-looking Northern Counties bodies. Even when parked against the kerb the first step looks to be a fair height. SJB

Above:

The Olympian, latterly a Volvo product, has been the definitive double-decker of the last 20 years, although Volvo's dominance of the double-deck bus business is under threat as operators switch to low-floor models. Capital Citybus operates both Leyland and Volvo Olympians with a range of bodies. A Northern Counties-bodied Volvo loads in Wood Green. SJB

So as new models arrived on the market, the perception was that a two-step entrance was acceptable. Thus the main 1980s chassis — Dennis Dominator, MCW Metrobus and Leyland Olympian — were all designed with two-step entrances in mind. The mid-engined Volvo Citybus — and Leyland's copy-cat Lion — showed how little concern there was, in some quarters at least, with getting floor heights down.

And so it continued until the 1990s, when access to public transport for disabled travellers became an issue. This initially produced a plethora of new single-deck models which met with varying degrees of success.

The pioneers were Neoplan, Scania and Dennis. Neoplan produced its N4014, which first entered UK service in Merseyside in May 1993. It was expensive. Scania adapted its N113, retaining the original drive train but adding a low frame and independent front suspension to produce the MaxCi — a catchy name to the Swedes, one assumes, if not to those of us living in countries with a more pithy approach to naming things. The MaxCi was soon forgotten, although the FlexCi which followed it, based on the L113, would be developed but without its

unfortunate choice of name. Dennis likewise adapted its Lance to produce the Lance SLF, unveiled at Coach & Bus 93 with Wright Pathfinder body. Dennis's SLF terminology — Super Low Floor — has come close to being a generic name for low-floor buses.

But these were cul-de-sacs off the super-highway of 1990s bus design. Operators were unwilling to pay a premium for the new models which, as well as being more expensive, actually provided fewer seats because as the floor was lowered wheel-arch intrusion took up more space. Wright of Ballymena, who was the key builder of low-floor buses at this time, argued with limited success that over the 15-year life of a bus the extra cost

45

of an accessible vehicle would be covered by increased revenue from additional passengers.

The model which made low-floor buses acceptable was the Dennis Dart SLF. It came to lead a market in which the main rivals were the Scania Axcess-ultralow (another catchy name from the Swedes, but at least better than FlexCi), Volvo's B10L (expensive), B10BLE, and B6LE — the last named superseded in 1999 by the B6BLE as Volvo juggled with letters and layouts as it tried to challenge Dennis' supremacy in this market segment.

Other players were MAN and Mercedes, the former supplying Stagecoach (no doubt to the chagrin of established supplier Volvo) and the latter supplying Travel West Midlands (no doubt to the chagrin etc…).

The appearance of new accessible models wasn't driven purely by the altruism of bus operators. A growing number of tendering authorities were insisting on accessible buses, following London's lead in 1992. And operators themselves were finding that low-floor buses really could generate new business, not just from disabled

people but from parents with baby buggies or elderly people with shopping trolleys. Indeed not all low-floor buses of the late 1990s have in fact been wheelchair-accessible, which was one of the aims of the original designs.

The other cause of change was the Disability Discrimination Act. The DDA covers a wide range of accessibility issues, one of which is ensuring that disabled travellers can use buses and trains. Its requirements are being phased in, and as far as bus operators are concerned the key issues are that most single-deck buses have to be wheelchair-accessible from January 2000, and all double-deckers from January 2001. There then follows a 15-year period during which buses with two- or three-step entrances have to be phased out of regular service. This reflects the normal theoretical lifespan of an urban bus — although in parts of the country where 20-year-old Atlanteans are still in operation this may be hard to believe.

So, in 1998, some of the last two-step single-deckers entered service in the UK. These included Alexander-bodied Volvo B10Ms for Stagecoach and Wright-bodied Volvo B10Bs for Harrogate & District. A handful of stock two-step single-deckers are expected to bring UK sales of the type to an end in 1999. Also in 1999 the last two-step double-deckers will take to Britain's streets.

Some models had in fact disappeared earlier. The last Dennis Arrows, with East Lancs Pyoneer bodies, went to Capital Citybus in the summer of 1998. The last of the original two-step Optare Spectras entered service in 1999. The Scania N113 will also disappear in 1999.

Below:

Iveco's ill-fated TurboCity 100 — a double-deck body on a single-deck chassis — had a relatively high floor. The split-step entrance — first seen on rear-entrance Lodekkas operated by Brighton Hove & District in the 1960s — was intended to make access easier for less agile passengers. Alexander built the body, with the front incorporating parts from Iveco's standard Italian city bus of the period. After a period as a demonstrator the TurboCity 100 was sold to Filers of Ilfracombe. Iveco

Above:
At the start of 1998 Alexander switched production of full-sized single-deckers from the high-floor PS-type to the low-floor ALX300. The last customer for the PS was Stagecoach. Most PS bodies were built on Volvo B10M chassis, as seen here with Stagecoach Manchester. SJB

Left:
DAF entered the double-deck market in 1991 with the DB250. The first chassis were bodied by Optare, but later the DB250 was made available with Northern Counties Palatine II bodies. A London Central Optare Spectra rounds Trafalgar Square with the National Gallery behind. SJB

Production of the market-leading double-decker, the Volvo Olympian, will also cease in 1999. Some of the last UK examples entered service in London in the spring, although Olympians may still be entering service in Dublin in the year 2000.

New-generation low-floor double-deck chassis have been launched by three manufacturers. First off the mark was DAF, with a low-floor DB250 which was exhibited at Coach & Bus 95. All then went quiet for two years, until the launch of the new low-floor Optare Spectra two years later at Coach & Bus 97. The first low-floor 'decker to enter passenger service was a Spectra running for A-Bus in Bristol in January 1998, just beating Travel West Midlands, Travel Dundee and Bullocks of Cheadle, all of whom had Spectras in service in the early part of the year, to be followed in the summer by Wilts & Dorset.

The only other low-floor 'deckers to enter service in 1998 were also based on DAF DB250LF chassis, but with Alexander ALX400 bodies. These were for operation by Arriva London North.

Further DAFs entered service in the early part of 1999 with Arriva in London and with Capital Logistics, which took over a London Transport contracted service using DB250LFs with Optare Spectra and Plaxton President bodies.

While DAF may have won the race, and by a handsome margin, it is Dennis which has secured the biggest orders. Dennis has in fact been supplying low-floor three-axle Tridents to Hong Kong since mid-1997, but its first UK-specification two-axle models only started to enter service in 1999. Incidentally, the two-axle Trident is not, say Dennis, to be called the Trident II, although they may find themselves overwhelmed by popular usage as operators, bodybuilders and enthusiasts use the obvious way to distinguish between two- and three-axle models.

The first Trident II — oops, two-axle Trident — was actually completed at the end of 1998 for Nottingham City Transport, with East Lancs' new low-floor derivative of its Pyoneer, appropriately called the Lolyne: the Dennis Loline rides again. It was followed by Tridents with Alexander ALX400 bodies for Stagecoach's London operations, and with Plaxton President bodies for Metroline.

The third chassis maker, Volvo, has been UK's double-deck market leader since taking over Olympian production from Leyland back in 1988. That is a position it is about to lose, as Trident orders are currently running well ahead of orders for what has appeared as the B7L.

An unnamed prototype, with an in-line engine mounted at the nearside rear, was shown at Coach & Bus 97, fitted with Plaxton's new Wigan-built President body. The body was acclaimed as the star of the show, with its striking interior layout (since imitated by some of Plaxton's rivals), but the chassis didn't meet with quite the same enthusiasm. It was in essence a European-style single-deck chassis, and Volvo went back to the drawing board to announce in mid-1998 a new version with a transverse rear engine which answered operators' criticisms of the overall length of the prototype and of its excessive rear overhang.

The first of the new B7L chassis was delivered to Plaxton Wigan — as Northern Counties had become — in late 1998, with two pre-production vehicles being completed early in 1999.

Every silver lining has a cloud, and with fully-accessible double-deckers that cloud is lower-deck seating capacity. The first dual-door DAFs for Arriva's London operation were 62-seaters with just 17 seats in the lower deck. Of these, only four were accessible without negotiating the step ahead of the rear axle. Which means that all of this design development to eliminate steps brought with it a reduction in lower-deck seating capacity and provided only four step-free seats.

The situation is much better in single-door buses, but the upshot is that if you want a seat on a low-floor double-decker in London there is a fair chance that you will find yourself climbing more steps rather than fewer,

Right:
The Dennis Dart SLF was the bus which played the biggest part in killing off single-deckers with two-step entrances. The Dart is Britain's best-selling bus. In recent years most have been bodied by Plaxton. This is a First Western National SLF with Plaxton Pointer body in Plymouth. SJB

because most of the seats are upstairs — although the situation will clearly be better for bus users outside London.

And that in turn really does call into question the usefulness of the double-decker, a type now rare outside the British Isles and Hong Kong.

The top decks are susceptible to vandalism. They are difficult to reach if you are laden with shopping, accompanied by children or just plain unsteady on your feet. In some towns care has to be taken not to send double-deckers under low bridges. On rural routes they can be damaged by overhanging branches.

The alternative? Articulated buses. It would be a braver man than I who would dare forecast the double-decker's demise and the artic's ascendancy. But there are signs that change might be on the way.

Articulated buses were first tried in Britain by the South Yorkshire PTE in 1979, following the inspection in 1977-8 of left-hand-drive demonstrators from Leyland DAB and Volvo by a number of UK operators.

SYPTE bought 10 — five Leyland DABs with bodywork built by Leyland National, and five MANs. After a relatively short spell in Sheffield some of the artics saw further service elsewhere — in particular, two of the Leyland-DABs with McGill of Barrhead, and the five MANs with Midland Red North. Further artics — seven Leyland DABs and three left-hand-drive Mercedes were bought for airport use — and South Yorkshire later took 13 Leyland DABs complete with DAB's own bodywork. These entered service in 1985.

Top:
The first of the new generation of fully-accessible double-deckers to enter service was this DAF with Optare Spectra bodywork running for A-Bus of Bristol. Lower floors have in most cases meant lower overall height, giving accessible double-deckers a distinctive squat appearance when seen head on. SJB

Above:
By early 1999 all four double-deck bus bodybuilders in the UK had low-floor models on offer. From Northern Counties — renamed Plaxton Wigan at the start of the year — came the President. Bonded glazing provided a modern appearance, but gasket-mounted windows were offered as an alternative. This is the first production President body on a DAF chassis, for Capital Logistics. SJB

INITIAL UK ORDERS FOR LOW-FLOOR DOUBLE-DECKERS

DAF DB250	ALEXANDER ALX400	OPTARE SPECTRA	PLAXTON PRESIDENT
A-Bus, Bristol		1	
Arriva Group	130		20
Bullocks		2	
Capital Logistics		6	10
Travel Dundee		1	
Travel West Midlands		21	
Wilts & Dorset		6	
Total DAF: 197			

DENNIS TRIDENT	ALEXANDER ALX400	EAST LANCS LOLYNE	PLAXTON PRESIDENT
Brighton & Hove		20	
First Capital			22
First CentreWest			31
Lothian			5
Metroline			65
Nottingham		12	
Oxford Bus Company	20		
Stagecoach group	100		
Yellow Buses		9	
Total Dennis: 284			

VOLVO B7L	ALEXANDER ALX400	PLAXTON PRESIDENT
London Central	46	
London General	45	
Lothian		1
Travel West Midlands		101
Total Volvo: 193		

BODYBUILDER TOTALS

Alexander	341
East Lancs	41
Optare	37
Plaxton	255

All then went quiet on the artic bus front — although Stagecoach and Ulsterbus have made limited use of artic coaches. But 1999 sees 51 articulated buses enter service in Britain. Forty of these are for FirstGroup and are Wright-bodied Volvos. The remaining 11 are Mercedes-Benz for Travel West Midlands. All are, of course, fully-accessible low-floor models.

They carry more people than a double-decker — 140 — but with fewer seats, although the vast majority of the seats — 55 in the FirstGroup buses — are easily accessible. An artic can, in theory, operate over any route traversed by a conventional 12m single-decker. But it does occupy considerably more road space than a double-decker, with its overall length of around 18m. In some depots designed around the needs of rear-engined buses of 9.5m overall length there could be problems in fitting extra-long buses into workshops and wash bays.

For those who baulk at the artic's size, it has to be borne in mind that they are operated successfully in many continental European cities where general driving standards and traffic congestion are little different from those in British cities.

Sales of double-deckers in Britain have fallen dramatically over the last two decades — they peaked in 1980 when almost 2,300 entered service, but have averaged around just 500 in the last few years. The double-decker is an efficient people-mover. It has survived the attack of the deregulated minibus. It has benefited from attractive restyling in the late 1980s and early 1990s — the Spectra, the Palatine II, the Royale, the Cityzen.

While cities like Edinburgh and London have, so far, remained loyal to double-deckers, operators in many more places have in the 1990s put into service unprecedented numbers of single-deckers: Aberdeen; Birmingham, Glasgow, Leeds, Liverpool, Manchester and Newcastle are just a few which immediately come to mind.

The Disability Discrimination Act and renewed interest in artics may just be fresh tests of the double-decker's resilience, but the signs are clear: its dominance of the urban transport scene is over. For ever.

LOSS OF LOCAL COLOUR

Consolidation of the bus industry is leading to a loss of variety; with the help of Tony Moyes we consider another recent loss in Wales, where Davies of Pencader disappeared in the summer of '99

It is ironic that the release of new entreprenurial talent as a result of the deregulation of the bus industry was not helpful to the old entreprenurial talent. Prior to deregulation and privatisation, the British bus industry may have been dominated by the public sector, but throughout Britain there was a significant, colourful and varied independent bus sector.

There were particular areas where they thrived, often in the 'fringes' of the country; Cornwall, East Anglia, Herefordshire, those parts of the north-east of England and of Yorkshire between the territories of the big operators — and of course Wales. All too often these efficient smaller operators, frequently passed down through generations of the same family, have been easy prey either to newcomers to the industry or to the burgeoning big groups. It has to be said that previous styles of Government policy on the bus industry didn't do much to help them either; think of all those independents swallowed up into the coffee and cream uniformity of South Yorkshire PTE, for instance.

One of the most recent to succumb has been the South West Wales independent Davies Bros (Pencader), which was put into receivership on 10 June 1999. KPMG was appointed as receiver and fortunately decided to continue to run things unchanged, with the hope of selling it as a going concern. The *Carmarthen Journal* of 16 June quoted the joint administrator as saying that '20 national and local bus companies were interested in buying the company', which had 90 staff and 60 vehicles. Debts of £3m were being talked of. Given the recent history of the company it is ironic that it was finally bought by the big local operator, First Cymru, perhaps better known by its earlier name of South Wales Transport.

Working a commercial town service in Carmarthen, Davies Bros (Pencader) Leyland Tiger/East Lancs 228 (A71 VTX) makes for the town centre on August 1995. The vehicle began its life with Inter Valley Link before being sold off in 1989 by National Welsh.

51

Davies had registered increasing amounts of its stage work as commercial to deter other entrants, and quoted highly competitive tenders for Dyfed County Council work. It had expanded greatly from its original base in Pencader and its focus on the Carmarthen-Lampeter route — run since the Davies Brothers had taken over the route in 1926 — and its Pencader-Llandysul feeder. In 1978 it picked up (inter alia) Carmarthen-Llandeilo and Carmarthen town services from Dan Jones, along with that company's modernised depot on Abergwili Road, Carmarthen. At deregulation, the traditional Davies routes were put up for tender in a package also incorporating Crosville's Lampeter-Aberaeron operation, which Davies won. In 1988, the large business of Eynon of Trimsaran came into Davies's net, and operations from Carmarthen and Trimsaran were registered to the subsidiary Davies

Bros (Carmarthen) Ltd. The enlarged business was successful in winning enhanced tendered services in the Carmarthen-Llanelli corridor in September 1990, and picked up virtually all of the former Crosville Cymru tendered trunk service between Carmarthen and Cardigan. It simultaneously lost the tendered journeys between Carmarthen, Lampeter and Aberaeron, and most of the tendered Carmarthen-Llandeilo-Llandovery route, to SWT.

At the next round of re-tendering in September 1994, Davies more than regained its losses from SWT, mostly at tender prices below those of 1990. However, quite suddenly on 2 March 1997, the company handed over the various routes worked by Trimsaran to SWT. Meanwhile the new counties of Carmarthenshire and Ceredigion had been looking at the level of support necessary to maintain

an hourly frequency on the Carmarthen-Cardigan service. After negotiation, Davies registered most of this service as commercial in April 1998, and at the same time picked up a little more tendered work on some minor rural routes at the expense of SWT and Meyers. Largely because of Davies's level of tendering, the amount of public support spent on the Carmarthen-Cardigan, Carmarthen-Aberaeron and Carmarthen-Llandovery axes in 1998 was well below that spent in 1986, for almost double the vehicle miles.

As a result another little dash of colour has been lost from South Wales, and the story reflects the irony of the situation whereby independents often pick up pieces discarded by bigger operators, only to lose out to them in the end.

Opposite
Davies took delivery of this East Lancs-bodied Dennis Dart (260: M260 VEJ) for the Cardigan service in May 1995. It is seen not long after entry into the fleet, leaving Carmarthen railway station.

Below
A Davies Bros line-up of schoolbuses at Pencader depot in July 1994 including two elderly Leyland Leopards bought new (Willowbrook-bodied LBX 549G and Plaxton-bodied NTH 119H) and 1971 ECW-bodied Daimler Fleetline UMS 97J, new to Alexander Midland.

Left:
Davies Bros (Pencader) had several Leyland Leopards rebodied by Willowbrook and re-registered in the early 1990s. One of these, 209 (FIL 7131), and Leyland Tiger 229 (A115 UDE) sandwich East Lancs-bodied Dennis Dart (260: M260 VEJ) at Carmarthen bus station in May 1995. Apparently the chassis of 229 had originally been a left-hand drive demonstrator.

Above:
Carmarthen bus station was reopened after refubishment in March 1999. In August 1994, however, the old layout involved a back road by which 222 (UKG475S) was leaving on a town service in September 1993.

Right:
One of the three 1990 Mercedes 709Ds, 234 (H881 EBX), near Ponthirwaun on a Cardigan-Carmarthen journey, August 1994.

A LAKELAND TALE For Grown-ups

David Holding warns of fierce creatures in the woods.

Beatrix Potter's 'Tale of Squirrel Nutkin' begins: 'This is a tale about a tail'. This is a tale about bus companies in the Lake District of Cumbria where Beatrix Potter wrote and set her stories. Like them, it has its marauding, wicked animals (so anyone of a nervous disposition should go to bed now), but it also has a Happy Ending. And unlike the Potter stories, this one is *true*. So are you sitting comfortably? Then I'll begin.

Once upon a time . . .

Once upon a time, the Lake District was divided territorially between two major companies. Cumberland (CMS) was a Tilling company, though rather an un-conventional one that preferred Leylands to Bristols into the 1950s, based in Whitehaven on the west coast. CMS had a depot in Keswick and others along the coastal strip, from which it covered the north-western side. Ribble, controlled by BET and based as now in Preston, had a long straggly Westmorland territory extending to Carlisle, where it ran most of the city services, but in between it covered the south-eastern Lakes from a depot at Ambleside and, like CMS, others at Kendal, Ulverston and Penrith which fed vehicles into the area.

There was only one joint service, the 74 from Keswick to Penrith, apart from which the two kept themselves to themselves. Both did well out of visitors travelling to the Lakes and from local movement, and they ran summer services into the remoter areas such as Buttermere (CMS) and over the Kirkstone Pass (Ribble).

The usual pattern of declining traffic was experienced during the 1960s to which the companies reacted with fare increases and minor service reductions, and as elsewhere the first serious appraisal was made as part of bargaining with county councils over subsidies in the early 1970s. Further rationalisation took place, particularly affecting Sunday and the seasonal services. The Kirkstone Pass service, which had seen three buses daily during the summer of 1968, was reduced to one trip on a Tuesday.

There was, however, a response to this. Members of the Taylor and Hudson families surmised that Ribble might not succeed running traditional buses in the

Top:
A Ford Transit of Mountain Goat, with added destination board and luggage rack, loads at Windermere Station in 1976 for the arduous Hardknott route to Wasdale
A. MOYES

Above:
Ribble's open-top Atlantean 1927 is seen here operating the 'Skyrider' service in Bowness durimg Spring Bank Holiday 1987 — but the destination display is less than helpful.
G. B. WISE

traditional way, but minibuses operated on a visitor-friendly basis could, and so Mountain Goat was born. Initially it concentrated on stage services into the areas which CMS and Ribble had abandoned, although it also began a new route westwards from Windermere to Wasdale. Before long the Taylors realised there were greater opportunities in day and half day tours, using minibuses to penetrate the remoter valleys and offering holiday packages including a selection of these tours. The stage services continued but were henceforward a minor part of the business.

Shock to the system

The next shock to the system was deregulation and privatisation. Both CMS and Ribble had of course been NBC subsidiaries since 1968 but had continued to go their own way except for minor tidying-up. In the days of 'big is beautiful' it had been rumoured that the 160-bus CMS would disappear into Ribble, and similar events elsewhere (eg Devon General) made this seem likely. The reason it never happened was probably that even in NBC's worst years CMS consistently turned in a profit; if it ain't broke, why fix it? It may even be that the later trend to smaller units followed recognition that companies like CMS and Southern Vectis actually did better.

Between 1980 and 1986 an intermediate regime existed where aspiring operators were to be granted Road Service Licences unless an objector produced convincing evidence that they should not. This had only isolated effects, but NBC appreciated, with the 'Trial Areas' running simultaneously, that the political wind was moving towards deregulation. One operator who gained licences during this period, John Yeowart, was permitted to introduce Whitehaven town services that competed with CMS. It had always been argued that a monopoly on profitable town routes was needed to cross-subsidise rural areas, and CMS reacted by taking off some rural services, including Cockermouth-Buttermere. The circulation of an NBC video focusing on these withdrawals gives grounds for suspicion that they were political rather than financially unavoidable — warning the Government of the effects of urban deregulation. Nonetheless, of course, deregulation went ahead. But before that, in 1985 CMS also took off its Keswick-based trips to Penrith, leaving Ribble to run a sketchy service from the other end on what had been a more-or-less hourly frequency. Then, as part of the 'equalisation' process, supposedly to break NBC up into units that would not be excessively large, it was decreed that Ribble's Carlisle and Penrith depots (the most northerly) should be transferred to CMS. When this took place in February 1986, at a stroke the CMS fleet increased by 50% — and it got the 74 back again.

After deregulation Lancaster City Transport made an ill-judged attack on Kendal and a couple of trunk routes in the southern Lakes, aided and abetted by Barrow Borough Transport, but Ribble proved too much for both of them and eventually absorbed not just the new ventures but the entire operations of both. Apart from this, the important issues were privatisation and county revenue support. Ribble initially passed to a management buy-out, but CMS went to the infant Stagecoach and on the following Friday its MD, the late Michael Wadsworth, found himself the possessor of a UB40. Cumbria CC then began a process of reducing its revenue support, which before deregulation had exceeded £1m a year, to the lowest level of any English county. By 1988 it was £290,000, in 1989 £152,000 and it fell to £141,000 in 1990/91. Some of this was destined for rail (the county is a keen supporter of the Settle-Carlisle line) and most of that allocated to buses went to the eastern and southern parts of the county. In fact the only services supported in the Lakes were postbuses, so the conventional network became entirely commercial, although in practice the county was still heavily involved through its payment for school travel.

The National Park Authority had supported Mountain Goat routes, but this came to an end too in 1987. At least it could be said that everybody knew where they stood, but it was not a happy time for buses in the Lakes and services reached their lowest level.

Cumberland decided with effect from August 1989 to close Keswick depot and bus station, which were too big for current levels of operation, and sell the site for redevelopment. This upset the Lake District planners, whose control over development was notoriously tight, but they had reckoned without the Stagecoach factor. The Cumberland property also included a parking ground used by visiting coaches during the season, which was filled with rusting hulks politely described as the Stagecoach 'reserve fleet'. Not only was this an eyesore to affront the planners but it shut out the visiting coaches, which had to be directed to a layby outside the town — to the annoyance of the police and local traders. The message from Stagecoach was clear; 'You can stand in the way of us developing our property, but you can't tell us how to use it in the meantime'. A deal was then, of course, agreed, under which the parking ground was kept and the rest of the site developed as a supermarket, leaving a small but adequate bus station which was opened in 1991.

Turning point

The turning point, ironically, was the decision of Ribble's management to 'cash in its chips' and sell to Stagecoach in April 1989. Almost immediately, in June, the remaining Ribble Cumbrian operations, compromising the depots at Kendal, Ulverston and Barrow, were transferred to Cumberland. The sale to Stagecoach did not include Ambleside bus station and depot, which remained in the hands of Ribble management and were closed in May with a view to redevelopment.

However, this proved a tougher nut than Keswick. Powerful local opposition to the retail development proposed (mainly on grounds of the traffic it would generate in the already congested town centre) delayed planning approval until 1996 and meanwhile it stood empty — almost as great an eyesore as the Keswick 'reserve fleet'. However, Cumberland continues to base five vehicles in an Ambleside car park which serves as an outstation.

But the good news was that one company, Cumberland, now ran virtually everything in the Lakes. Its town routes in Carlisle, Barrow, Workington and Whitehaven were profitable and it could afford to experiment. Management in Perth strongly encouraged internal, organic growth, territorially the company had nowhere to go, with sea on three sides and the inhospitable North Pennines to the east, so the obvious area to develop was the Lakes. Near-monopoly (the opposite, of course, of deregulation's intended effect) also encouraged area-wide planning, fares promotions and publicity. Ribble had introduced a newspaper-style free publication for its Lakes services, which was developed and enhanced by Cumberland. Now with the benefit of financial support from the County, the Friends of the Lake District and advertising, the *Lakeland Explorer* has since 1996 become a much more attractive colour publication including bus-based walks.

The first major initiative was on the only real urban services within the Lakes, linking the towns of Bowness, Windermere and Ambleside and running alongside Lake Windermere. These had been run by Ribble with conventional saloons and converted to Mercedes 608s as Minilink W1-W3 in 1986. In 1987 Ribble had acquired an open-top Atlantean originally with Devon General and ran it over the same route under the 'Skyrider' title. The idea was noted by Mountain Goat who acquired another open-

Right:
Bank holiday and it's raining in the Lakes. At Windermere station in 1987 a Ribble National holds back while 'Minilink' Mercedes 532 takes on its soggy load.
G. B. WISE

topper (a Fleetline) for a 'Lakeland Shuttle' in 1989. The Taylors arranged a co-ordinated timetable and fares with the ferry operators on Windermere, whereby the Fleetline would meet the ferry at its northern Waterhead terminal and then run north through Ambleside to Grasmere.

Southdown of the north

Taylor's service, however, followed the same route as Ribble's long-standing trunk 555 (Lancaster-Kendal-Ambleside-Keswick); Ribble might have stood for it but the new regime wouldn't. In a classic piece of Stagecoachery four open-top VRTs were transferred from Southdown, given a fresh coat of the traditional apple-green livery, and used to operate the entire W1-W3 service for the summer of 1990 along with similarly-painted Atlantean 1927.

Mountain Goat was suitably deterred from competing but sold the idea to Guide Friday, which began operating a week after the VRTs. Its service, advertised in Mountain Goat publicity, followed the Guide Friday pattern of offering a Day Ticket for unlimited travel at £3.50, but it failed to make an impact. For 1995 the VRT 'Lakeland Experience' service (renumbered 599) was extended to Grasmere, using a further Cumberland VRT which had conveniently met an obstruction; the original Atlantean was also replaced by a similar model originating in Portsmouth. The 599 meets North West Trains arrivals at

Windermere station, where at times 80 or more passengers can present themselves for onward travel. This is encouraged by a Lakes Day Tripper which includes unlimited bus travel on arrival from centres such as Liverpool and Manchester.

Equally important, the green livery was thought so attractive and appropriate to the Lakes that it has been adopted for other tourist-oriented services as they have been developed; thus as apple green has disappeared from Sussex, a Southdown enclave has spread in Cumbria and the livery applied with route-based branding to 608s, 709s, a Leyland National B, an Olympian and Volvo B6s.

With one of these routes, branded the 'Coniston Rambler' (505/506), it must again be admitted that competition was the spur. In the 1980s the service had declined to a point where it seemed likely that Coniston would be left without any buses at all, then Lakes Supertours (F. & S. Jones of Windermere) registered a service to run from Bowness to Hill Top (Beatrix Potter's house), branding it the Peter Rabbit Route. Again CMS responded by registering a parallel service, but extending it to run as a circular including Coniston, and this had the required deterrent effect. It now runs hourly on weekdays from March to October with extra journeys in the summer and up to six trips on Sundays. Many Passengers are Japanese, the explanation being that Beatrix Potter's stories are the medium used to teach English to Japanese children!

North and west of Keswick

Our next case study follows the east-west A66 corridor from Workington through Keswick to Penrith. This was strategically important, because Keswick had lost its rail service in 1972 and henceforward access to the capital of the Northern Lakes was by bus from Penrith (on the West Coast Main Line), the bus passing the rail station on its way out. Nonetheless, following CMS's opt-out in 1985 the service might have disappeared had OK Travel of Bishop Auckland not expressed interest in diverting its Darlington-Carlisle service at Penrith to Keswick. CMS did not relish OK involvement in the Lakes and agreed a connecting service with through fares across Penrith.

To the west of Keswick an hourly 35/36 from Whitehaven and Cockermouth had fallen to around six journeys; by 1992 the Keswick-Penrith (now numbered 105) had increased to the same level and from 1993 the two were combined to form 'Lakeslink' service X5, running Whitehaven-Penrith. An hourly March-October service has now been established, running as Stagecoach Express X4/X5. Sundays originally had no service but since 1994 a timed interchange has been provided. This involves X4, X5, the 555 from Lancaster which also has three journeys projected northwards to Carlisle, and then 77 and 79 into Borrowdale which are discussed next.

The 79 runs south from Keswick to terminate at Seatoller, at the foot of the Honister Pass. For many

years it was operated jointly by CMS and four local operators to a highly complex rotational system reminiscent of the A1 partnership in Ardrossan, but the last of the private operators (who traded as Keswick-Borrowdale Bus Services) sold out to CMS in 1967. Its popularity with tourists is shown by a frequency in a mountainous valley which in those days sometimes reached every 20 minutes. It was promoted vigorously by Michael Wadsworth, who produced a route leaflet and claimed the title for it 'The most beautiful bus ride in England'. He might had added 'and the wettest'; Borrowdale is alleged to enjoy 120 inches of rain a year. In 1980 79 was running hourly and fell after deregulation to less than a daily service. By 1992 the hourly summer frequency had been restored and apple green applied to 810, a Leyland National B-series of Penrith depot, together with a 'Borrowdale Bus' logo.

Experiments with new services to the west of Keswick then followed, which settled down as 77 to Buttermere, the 'Honister Rambler'. This uses a green Mercedes 709, which, following the removal of a restriction on the use of minibuses over Honister Pass, now runs as a circular four times daily and supplements the 79 to Seatoller over a route taking the western rather than the eastern shore of Derwentwater. On the 79 itself Cumberland was able in 1996, following some tree-pruning activity, to defy Borrowdale's watery reputation and replace the National by a spare open-top VRT. For the 1997 season 2076 was, with funding from the Department of transport under its 'Cycle Challenge' initiative, fitted with a rear-end cycle rack so that cyclists would be encouraged to take the bus along the tortuous road rather than cycle — or, frequently, carry the cycle strapped to a car.

The Goat retreats

What of Mountain Goat? While CMS and Ribble concentrated on their 'core' routes there was room for a leisure-oriented small operator, but once Cumberland management realised the opportunities for using spare buses and drivers at weekends and during school holidays, conflict was bound to follow. Evidently bruised by its experience with the 'Lakeland Shuttle', Mountain Goat in 1990 also withdrew from Keswick-Patterdale (which Cumberland restored as 37 in 1996), and in 1991 ceased running over Kirkstone Pass from Ambleside to Glenridding. This was revived for 1993, but meanwhile Cumberland's 77 was nibbling at Mountain Goat traffic on its remaining Keswick-Buttermere service.

In 1994 Cumberland registered its 517 'Kirkstone Rambler' from Bowness to Glenridding, and this was the final straw for Mountain Goat, which having originally intended to run both services then deregistered them. The business changed hands soon afterwards and its new owners have wisely concentrated on the tours where Mountain Goat has a national reputation.

An unusual successor is the National Trust, which is a major landowner in the Lakes and under a new Director-General has been concerned to reduce the proportion of visitors to its properties who use cars. As part of its 100th anniversary celebrations in 1995, the Trust introduced a free minibus service on Sundays from Keswick to Watendlath, a side valley which experiences serious traffic problems but where attempts to restrict cars have been frustrated. In the following year a further service was introduced from Hawkshead to Tarn Hows, another popular spot not served by public transport. The Watendlath service partly duplicates the 79 and led to some initial skirmishing with Cumberland, but seems now to be accepted, while the Tarn Hows service connects in Hawkshead with 505/506 timings.

Opposite above:
Windermere station has been attractively redeveloped to incorporate a bus-rail interchange. In May 1987, Ribble coach-seated Olympian 2176 circles before tackling a substantial queue outside the supermarket which now occupies the old station building.
G. B. WISE

Opposite below:
CAO 505, a 1937 Ford BB with Willetts 20-seat body, was owned by R. W. Simpson of Keswick, one of the partners in Keswick-Borrowdale Bus Services. It shows some similarity to Swiss Saurer postbuses of the same period.
R. C. DAVIS

Above:
A later acquisition for the same route, a Commer Q4 of 1948 owned by Weightmans Ltd waits at the Moot Hall, Keswick, stand used by the Keswick-Borrowdale independents. The body was by Myers & Bowman of Distington (about 20 miles west of Keswick), the Commer main agent at the time.
R. C. DAVIS

Happy Ending

I promised you a Happy Ending. Part of it must be that bus companies can expand the market without subsidy and attract customers out of cars if they go about it professionally; Cumberland believes many of the visitors attracted to these seasonal services have arrived in the area by car.

Secondly, it isn't a 'flash in the pan'. Services have been developed steadily since 1992 and virtually all have performed well enough to justify continuation and expansion the next year. Since the closure of Ambleside and Keswick depots, Kendal has borne the brunt of the seasonal services, and the point has now been reached where it cannot cope and drivers are borrowed from Morecambe (though it is a sad reflection on the decline of that resort that it has spare drivers during the summer holiday period!). As commercial Sunday services disappear in other parts of the country, here they are being reintroduced, increased and the season extended.

One exception to the track record of success is services from Barrow-in-Furness, which is a large industrial town with low car ownership and poor access to the rest of the UK. Logically it should be easy to maintain an operation into the Lakes, but in practice the service fell from hourly in summer 1968 to a very sketchy connecting facility after 1994. However, a determined effort has been made since 1997. Currently an occasional X18 operates Barrow-Ambleside and X12 runs Coniston-Ulverston (connecting from Barrow every 90min.

Lastly, Cumbria CC has come back into the picture. Between 1992 and 1995 a Traffic Management Initiative project examined the traffic problems of the Lake District, with representation from the county, the National Park, the Countryside Commission and the Cumbria Tourist Board. The project ended in serious dissent between the parties as to the measures necessary, but one thing on which they could agree was the need to improve public transport. As a result, county revenue support has begun to increase again and stands at £236,000 for 1999/2000, plus £957,000 rural bus grant. The fact that a commercial network was already in place, including all the seasonal services mentioned (except X12) and others besides, meant that the county could use its new funds to experiment and develop. In 1994, a 'Kentmere Rambler', partly funded by the Friends of the Lake District, brought a summer weekend service to a valley which had last seen a bus in 1971 and was experiencing problems with visitor parking; county funding has allowed the minibus used also to run 'socially necessary' services to other villages which had lost their buses. Together with Cumberland, the county has also been developing links between the Central Lakes and the Furness Coast around Grange-over-Sands, which has an elderly population, to improve mobility. An ambitious interchange between Kendal and Windermere is planned, involving bus and rail Park-&-Ride and also walking and cycling routes.

So you see, all the animals in the farmyard lived happily ever after — but I don't think any of them were cheeky to Mr McGregor again. Mr McGregor? For those, who have forgotten, he was the Scotsman who wanted to put Peter Rabbit in a pie for eating his lettuces.

Top:
Open-top Cumberland Bristol VRT 2076 (UWV 622S), as fitted to carry cycles on service 79 in Borrowdale.
D. HALLIDAY

Above:
Mercedes 709 78, liveried for 'Honister Rambler' and open-top 'Borrowdale Bus' VRT 2076 meet in Seatoller.
H. POSTLETHWAITE

TROLBUSSZAL
MENTEM
A TESCOBA
a Trail Through Two Cities

Michael Dryhurst compares and contrasts public transport in Budapest and San Francisco.

Courtesy of many years in the movie industry, I have done an enormous amount of travelling all over the world, in the process having seen some wonderful sights and visited many interesting cities. Like San Francisco. In 1969, I was the First Assistant Director on a 20th Century Fox production entitled *The Games*, which starred a (somewhat) youthful Michael Crawford; with the Olympic marathon as its background, this film was shot in London, Reading (yes, Reading!), Rome, Sydney and Tokyo.

Having completed the schedule in the Japanese capital, most of the crew returned east-west directly to London, but your scribe? Me, I went transpacific to Honolulu and then on to…San Francisco. A fascinating city, especially for the serious transport enthusiast, so much so that I was there again in 1970, after having been working on a film in Mexico. Moving from the UK to California and settling eventually in the north of 'The Golden State', San Francisco (to the cognoscenti never 'SF' nor worse yet, 'Frisco') is but 120 miles from where this piece is being written.

In 1989 I was the Co-Producer on the Bruce Willis movie *Hudson Hawk*, and was travelling in Europe seeking suitable locations. One such contender was the Hungarian capital, Budapest; after a further four exploratory visits we filmed there in 1990, when I was living in the city for some six weeks.

Christmas 1997 saw the lady wife Karen working in Budapest, where I joined her. As all of my previous visits had been while working and thus had precluded excursions, this latter stay afforded me the chance to go 'bussing', big time… And the more I rode around the Hungarian capital, the more I realised how much in common the public transport system of Budapest had with that of San Francisco.

Well, they say opposites attract… But they're so alike. Both are hilly, both operate buses, trams, trolleybuses, underground railways and suburban railways; both have their transport idiosyncrasies, in the case of San

Above:
Tatra trams, built in what was Czechoslovakia, approach a combined bus/tram/subway interchange. All BKV trams are either articulated or run in close-coupled sets. All photographs by the author

In the modern post-Soviet Union-dominated Hungary, the transport of the capital is in the hands of Budapesti Kozlekedesi Vallalat or Budapest Transport Co, the working acronym of which is BKV. BKV came into being on 1 January 1968, an amalgamation of various local transport entities.

Moving forward, less than a year after the inauguration in Glasgow of Britain's last trolleybus system, Fovarosi Villamosvasut put into service the first Budapest trolleybuses, on 21 December 1949. The Budapest trolleybus system reached its zenith in the 1980s, and while there are plans to reduce it, there is no intention (so it is said…) to scrap the BKV trolleybuses. By mid-1998 there was a fleet of some 182 trolleybuses, comprising Russian-built Uritsky ZIU9 two-axled buses and Ikarus 280T and 435T articulated trolleybuses plus the sole Ikarus Abus 411T two-axled prototype.

Livery is an interesting aspect of BKV operations, with particular types of vehicle wearing an individual colour scheme, viz motorbuses blue/grey, trolleybuses red/grey, trams yellow, cog railway red/white, suburban railway green/white; on the Metro, each line (M1, M2, M3) has an individual livery with the cars being painted accordingly.

While the Hungarian railway system is relatively comprehensive and participates in many international services, most interurban and international travel is by coach; within Hungary this is provided by the Ibusz and Volanbusz networks, plus franchised bus services associated with the State railway. Volanbusz, with its Communist-era livery, is the main long-distance operator but in recent years its fleet complement has changed dramatically, with the standardised coach version of the Ikarus 280 having given way to Volvo B10M and Scania, although these new vehicles carry bodywork by Ikarus, albeit to a much-improved specification and look.

In addition to Ibusz and Volanbusz there are a number of international services, particularly between Budapest and Vienna, and when I was in Budapest in 1989, a city sightseeing tour was being run with an ex-United Counties Bristol VRT in an all-over red livery, while I found a local church using an ex-Greater London Council Bedford VAS. But neither was apparent at Christmas 1997, only a Routemaster in use as a playbus at a suburban Budapest McDonalds.

Some 7,000 miles west of Budapest lies San Francisco, in California; the whole of the San Francisco region is known as the Bay Area, which locality is regarded as having the best public transport facilities in the American west, certainly in California. Within the City and County of San Francisco, local transport is provided by the San Francisco Municipal Railway (Muni), with its buses, cable cars, light-rail, streetcars and trolleybuses.

Like Budapest, San Francisco boasts an underground system but this is nothing to do with Muni. The San Francisco Bay Area Rapid Transit District (BART) is a 95-mile network serving four counties in the core of the Bay Area, its trains being made up from a fleet of 669 cars; an interesting aspect of BART is that the track gauge is 5ft 6in, being an early design feature to ensure stability of lightweight rolling stock. While the BART system

Francisco its cable cars, and in Budapest, the cog railway, each of which commenced within a year of the other. Furthermore, the two cities are linked by disaster — earthquakes and fire in San Francisco; war, invasion and a brutally-crushed revolution in the case of Budapest. Plus the fact that in both cities there is extensive use of both buses and trolleybuses in articulated form.

Originally in Hungary there were two cities. One, west of the Danube, was Buda, that to the east of the river…Pest. Administratively they were linked in 1872, horse-drawn omnibuses and trams having taken to the streets respectively in 1866 and 1868. In 1887 the first electric trams were operated in Budapest, while its subway, opened in 1896, was the second such electrified system in the world, after London. The first motorbuses appeared seasonally in 1909, permanent service being implemented in 1911.

commenced operations in 1972, its Budapest counterpart pre-dates it by some 76 years.

But back to buses. Muni has the largest trolleybus fleet in North America and apart from a couple of preserved US-built examples in its heritage fleet, the Muni trolleybus fleet is 100% Canadian — some 340 Flyer E800 two-axled buses and 60 New Flyer E60 articulated vehicles. Although BKV in Budapest has a third more articulated trolleybuses than Muni, its total trolleybus fleet at the beginning of 1998 was but 182, less than half that of San Francisco. The main reason for this is that Muni has been converting a number of motorbus routes to trolleybus operation, hence the large intake of artics in 1994/5.

Perhaps the most interesting comparison of trolleybus operation in the two cities is that, in the main, BKV employs its trolleybuses in flat Pest, on relatively short routes with intensive headways, whereas Muni uses its trolleybuses on some of the hilliest terrain in San Francisco. In the BKV operating area the hilliest territory is in Buda, and west of the Danube, but no BKV trolleybus routes cross the river. Plenty of tram services do (some twice), but no trolleybuses!

On the other hand, within Budapest's City Park there are two roads for trolleybus use exclusively, surely the most scenic such reservations anywhere. In San Francisco, there is a semblance of trolleybus reservation, in the heart of the Downtown area, where streetcars and trolleybuses share a central reservation on the famous Market Street.

The BKV bus fleet is standardised totally on the locally-built Ikarus, at one time the world's largest producer of buses. Since my first visit in 1989 there has been a considerable intake of new buses, with the Ikarus 435 replacing the older 280 model, and while many of the new 435s are powered by RABA engines, the more recent deliveries feature a DAF power-train, while the Ikarus 465 midibus is powered by a Perkins unit.

In January 1998, the BKV bus fleet totalled 1,453 vehicles, of which some 40% were articulated units. Articulated buses feature largely in the Muni fleet, too; in fact, of the four transit agencies working into San Francisco (Muni, AC

Transit, SamTrans and Golden Gate Transit), only the last named does not operate any such vehicles.

While for many years the Muni fleet was comprised solely of buses of US manufacture, this is no longer the case, despite the fact that Gillig buses are built the other side of the Bay, at Hayward. The vast majority of Muni buses are from Canadian manufacturer Flyer/New Flyer, in both rigid and articulated form, while there is a small midibus fleet comprising Orion Mk1 vehicles from the early 1980s. Additionally, there is a fleet of MAN articulated buses, although these were assembled in the US by the former American Motors, now part of the Chrysler group, which itself has merged recently with Daimler-Benz…

In fact, if buses are to qualify for supporting funds under the US Federal Transit Agency programme, they must have at least a 60% US content, thus the Canadian Flyer, New Flyer and Orion buses at work in the USA are assembled in that country rather than being imported from Canada as complete vehicles, despite the existence of the North America Free Trade Area, which legislation was approved by Canada, Mexico and the United States… bureaucracy gone mad!

Above right:
The SamTrans fleet includes 15 Volvo B10M artics. Volvo supplied both rigid and articulated B10Ms to operators in the USA during the 1980s from a plant in Virginia — 55 of the former and 175 of the latter.

Right:
Trolleybuses figure in the BKV fleet. These include over 80 Russian-built Uritsky ZIU9 vehicles. Note the set-back front door, dictated by the design of the driver's compartment which separates him completely from the passengers.

Top:
Grosvenor Bus Lines is the San Francisco franchisee for Gray Line and its fleet includes 10 Leyland Olympians with ECW bodywork.

Above:
A one-off in the BKV fleet is this experimental Ikarus Abus 411T trolleybus, a 25-seater in an eye-catching livery of orange and grey with a bright green front section. The standard trolleybus colours are deep red and grey.

On the tram side, while the BKV system has seen some contraction, particularly in both the inner and outer suburbs, the fleet numbers some 800 working units and although the tram fleet is but 55% of the BKV bus fleet, passenger loadings are 65% of the buses. This can be attributed to the intermodal connecting of the Metro and trams, with the latter then running into the heart of the Budapest business district with what are effectively trains of close-coupled articulated units, up to eight cars long in peak periods, travelling on city streets at speeds of up to 45mph (or more!), mass transit at its working best. And despite the tramway mileage reductions, BKV has no intention of scrapping the system; indeed, route 2 has been re-equipped recently with a fleet of new, very impressive, Ganz articulated trams.

On the other hand, San Francisco Muni has had a rethink tram-wise. All surface streetcar operation ceased in the early 1980s. A mammoth engineering project saw the Market Street routes put into a subway below street level but above the BART tunnels, emerging therefrom in the outer Downtown area, the revised system being dubbed Muni Metro and equipped with a new fleet of Boeing-Vertol light rail vehicles.

However, such was the dissatisfaction expressed at the loss of the surface streetcars that in 1995 the Transbay Terminal to Castro Street line, using Market Street for most of its length, was reinstated, the rolling stock being 1940s/1950s refurbished PCC cars, which had been purchased from a number of US cities. These trams are painted either in the livery of their previous owner or in the colours of a fleet that had used PCC cars, such as Pacific Electric.

Other Muni lines are being extended or introduced, particularly along the Embarcadero to Fisherman's Wharf or in the other direction, to Third Street, which has seen a London Docklands-type of renaissance, especially with residential development.

The Boeing-Vertol LRV cars have not been the most successful vehicles and are being replaced currently with a batch of similar vehicles built by the Italian firm of Breda, which carry a striking livery of silver and red.

And Muni has its cable cars, still. The original system is credited to one Andrew Hallidie, a Scotsman, who, upon seeing a heavily-laden horse-car roll backwards downhill pulling four terrified horses in its wake after one of the animals had slipped, decided there had to be a better way…

Three lines remain in operation (and if you don't want to wait in a lengthy queue to board one, ride the California Street line), and as old cars wear out new ones are built to replace them, albeit to the original 1873 design. Less than a year after Hallidie piloted the first cable car up a section of Clay Street in San Francisco, Budapest had in operation its cog railway, from Varosmajor suburb up into the hills 1,600ft above the city. Some 10 cars are in use, built in Austria by Brown Boveri. At its outer end the cog connects with the Children's

Railway, the narrow-gauge line that, except for drivers, is run exclusively by children, originally by the Communist Pioneer scouts, to prepare 'em young for a railway career.

Another Budapest/San Francisco similarity is ferries; both cities have ferry services, extensive in the Bay area.

But where there is a difference is that in Budapest BKV is the sole transit operator, whereas San Francisco, including BART, boasts five transit concerns running into the heart of the city.

From the east, mainly Oakland, comes AC (Alameda County) Transit, traversing the lengthy Bay Bridge and terminating at the Transbay Terminal. AC Transit was created out of the old Key System interurban streetcar network, which ran articulated sets across the Bay Bridge, AC Transit taking to the streets of Alameda County on 1 October 1960, with an initial fleet of 250 buses. By 1998 this had grown to 750 buses, of which a number are 60ft-long articulated units by New Flyer. Given that Hayward is in its operating area, AC Transit operates a large number of Gillig buses At the end of

Below:
The long-distance bus station in Budapest has been described by one local writer as 'a most poetic building of the short quiet period after 1945. Its special beauty is characteristic of Corbusier-style modernism'. Against that background, who would give the Ikarus-bodied Scania of Volanbusz a second glance?

1998, 44 low-floor buses were on order, and one assumes that these will be by Gillig as a) they are built locally and b) there is such a fleet in operation with Hertz at San Francisco International Airport. AC Transit operates a number of Champion, El Dorado and Supreme minibuses, while other full-sized vehicles are by Gillig, Flyer, New Flyer and North American Bus Industries, a relative newcomer to the scene and, in the opinion of your scribe, these NABI vehicles are amongst the best-looking transit buses in the United States.

Unlike the trend in Britain, where the mega groups are disposing of buses previously preserved, commendably AC Transit retains a heritage fleet of a 1955 and a 1958 GMC Old Look plus a 1960 GMC New Look Fishbowl. AC Transit livery is a white base, with orange and turquoise relief; sounds naff, looks great.

From the north into San Francisco runs Golden Gate Transit and, yes, it is part of the same organisation that is responsible for the famed Golden Gate Bridge. GG Transit came into being in 1970 and took to the road in December of that year, using five leased Greyhound buses on a route from the residential areas of Marin County to the ferry at Sausalito. Local bus service within Marin County commenced on 15 December 1971, while 17 days later, on 1 January 1972, basic bus service started across the Golden Gate Bridge, being followed two days later by commuter bus service replacing a Greyhound route; within a month of running this service, GG Transit was carrying an average of 5,500 commuters a day, compared with the Greyhound average of 3,500.

While not featuring any articulated vehicles, the current 269-strong fleet, all of which is lift-equipped to comply with the US Disabilities Act, comprises seven GMC RTS (out of an original batch of 51), 143 RTS but built by GMC, and a further 30 RTS, by now built by Nova. There are 41 Flxibles from 1994, based on the Grumman transit bus, and then 44 MCI coaches, and four Gillig 26-seat midibuses. Golden Gate Transit buses carry an attractive white and green livery, and the agency has preserved a 1972 GMC New Look from the original batch.

Lastly, from the south (no buses run into San Francisco from the west, only ships…) come the buses of the San Mateo County Transit District, under the operating name of SamTrans; as the name implies, the main operating area is the county of San Mateo but SamTrans runs a number of services into downtown San Francisco, perhaps the best known being the 7 group, which also serve San Francisco International Airport. While most of its rigid buses are of local Gillig manufacture, SamTrans operates a large fleet of articulated vehicles, by Flyer, New Flyer (in case it's not been mentioned previously, New Flyer was the successor to Flyer), Neoplan and Volvo. In fact, many of these artics are owned by Grosvenor Bus Lines of San Francisco and operated under contract to SamTrans, carrying that operator's white, red, blue and black livery (sounds naff, looks fine).

Grosvenor itself has the Gray Line franchise in San Francisco, owning 10 three-axled Eastern Coach Works-bodied Leyland Olympians, and recently was purchased by the group Coach USA.

And the other Budapest/San Francisco difference? Fare collection. While all of the Bay Area operators provide various passes, on-board ride purchase is available. In Budapest, all BKV travel is with prepaid tickets purchased at various off-vehicle sites, and the BKV vehicles are designed in such a way that although having a front entrance, the driving cab is full-width, featuring an angled wall from the steering-wheel area to the nearside front; there is a door in this wall giving the driver access to the cab, but the design is such that passengers are channelled away from the (non-fare-taking) driver.

Model-wise, I have never come across a replica of a BKV vehicle, but the Bay Area operators fare somewhat better. Corgi produces its GMC New Look in AC Transit

Below:
A new Ikarus midibus in the BKV fleet leaving the old city of Buda. It has a Perkins engine and small wheels which provide a low, but not step-free, floor.

colours, while in HO-scale is available the Road Champs Flxible in AC Transit livery; back to Corgi, and its magnificent PCC car is available in the earlier cream and green Muni livery.

In conclusion, for help with facts, figures and history, I wish to express my sincere thanks to Mary Currie of the Golden Gate Bridge, Highway and Transportation District, Mike Healy of BART, and Mike Mills of AC Transit for my Bay Area info. I was able to communicate easily in English with the above persons.

Not so for Budapest facts! So a humungous 'Koszonom' to Visnyovszky Tunde, for her truly invaluable help in obtaining the information I requested and then translating it into English. Without the aforementioned ladies and gents affording me their time, this piece would not have been possible.

Oh, and the title? (Thanks to Tunde!) 'I Took a Trolleybus to Tesco's'. Which I did. Several times. BKV Route 80, from Keleti station…

Above:
Seen laying over at Daly City is one of 60 Flyer E-60 articulated trolleybuses delivered to the Muni in San Francisco in 1993-4. These were additions to the fleet for use on routes previously served by diesel buses.

Below:
'Trolibusszal mentem a Tescoba…' A BKV Ikarus 435T artic illustrates the title of this feature, as it picks up outside a Tesco supermarket in suburban Budapest. Which proves that not all trolleys outside Tesco are wayward wire receptacles which are impossible to steer in a straight line back to your car…

FIVE*DE*

of Bus Photogra

CADES

hy

Michael Fowler started taking bus photographs in the 1950s, when he worked for Doncaster Corporation Transport, first as a trolleybus conductor and later as a driver, having taken his PSV driving test in a Leyland Tiger PS1 operated by Gem Coaches of Colsterworth.

Left:
1950s GLASGOW
New in 1953, this was one of 20 Sunbeam F4As operated by Glasgow Corporation. It had a 60-seat Weymann body.
All photographs are by the author

Below:
1950s DONCASTER
Seen near the racecourse, an unfrozen AEC Regent in the Doncaster Corporation fleet, which entered service in 1942. Roe built the body on this, as on most of Doncaster's buses.

Left:
**1960s
LONDON**
At the start of
1960s London
Transport still
operated an
extensive troll
system. Typica
the vehicles in
was this Metro
Cammell-bodi
three-axle AE
dating from 1
The location is
Kentish Town.

Above
1960s DONCASTER
Odd buses in the Sheffield Joint Omnibus Committee fleet were five Leyland Titan PD2s with ECW bodies. They were
new in 1957 at a time when virtually all of ECW's output was on Bristol chassis. This one is seen leaving Doncaster's
Waterdale bus station for its home city.

Left:
**1960s
CLEETHORPES**
Old half-cab coaches were often modernised either by fitting full-width fronts or, as on this Maudslay Marathon III, by fitting a new body — in this case a Duple Vega. It was being operated by Peter Sheffield Coaches of Cleethorpes, but had been new to RACS of London.

Below:
1970s CARDIFF
Cardiff's last half-cabs were Guy Arabs with Alexander bodies, which entered service in 1965-6. Two are seen in the fleet's 1970s orange livery in the city's bus station.

Below:
1970s SPALDING

The 1970s was the era of the National Bus Company and the uniformity which came with it. A contrast in ECW-bodied Bristols is provided in this view of a brand-new Lincolnshire Road Car VRT alongside a 10-year-old Eastern Counties FS.

Inset:
1970s MANCHESTER

It says Ribble in small letters on the side, but this white National coach could have belonged to virtually any of NBC's subsidiaries. It is a Leyland Leopard with Duple Dominant body, arriving in Manchester from East Lancashire on the X43 — a service still operated today by Stagecoach Ribble.

Right:
1980s LIVERPOOL
A reminder of the brief interest in urban standee buses of the late 1960s and early 1970s is this Metro-Scania of the Merseyside PTE. New in 1972, it was photographed at Liverpool Pier Head bus station 10 years later. Merseyside had 20 Metro-Scanias.

Below:
1980s BIRMINGHAM
A number of manufacturers challenged Leyland's supremacy of the double-deck market including Ailsa, with a front-engined model developed to pander to the conservatism of the Scottish Bus Group. The second biggest English buyer of Ailsas (after the South Yorkshire PTE) was the West Midlands PTE, with 53. They had Alexander bodies.

Above:
1980s LONDON
Competition on express services following 1980's coach deregulation saw National Express explore ways of improving service quality. Part of this exploration saw 10 rear-engined Dennis Falcons with Duple Goldliner bodies being tried out. This one was operated by Western National. The Falcons were not an unqualified success.

Above:
1990s BURY
New life for old Leyland Nationals was promised by East Lancs with its Greenway conversions which saw the basic (and sound) National structure being rebuilt with simplified heating, new panelling and the option of re-engining too. This Hyndburn bus started life as a National 2. It was among the buses acquired by Stagecoach when it took over Hyndburn's operations in 1996.

Above:
1990s SOUTH SHIELDS
Dennis, like Leyland, saw a market for a midibus and its response was the Dart, a considerably more successful
vehicle than the short-lived Swift. Catch A Bus was a post-deregulation bus operation started up by a coach
operator, Hylton Castle. This Dart has a Plaxton Pointer body, a best-selling combination in the mid-1990s. Catch A
Bus ceased operating in 1997.

Below:
1990s GRAYS
Harris of Grays, a respected coach operator, expanded into bus operation after bus deregulation in 1986. This was
Leyland's response to the perceived demand for a new breed of midibuses: the mid-engined Swift. It has a Wadham
Stringer Vanguard body.

TWENTY
YEARS IN ENFIELD

Enfield resident Peter Rowlands looks back
at two decades of change.

In the early 1980s Fleetlines were commonplace. One heads
south in Chase Side, observed by a horse looking out the first
floor window on the right. All photographs by the author

was fooled. House-hunting in Enfield that day in 1980, I caught the unmistakable sound of a Routemaster passing somewhere nearby. Through heavy summer foliage from an upstairs window I glimpsed the bus making its way north up Chase Side.

Well, if Routemasters ran here — getting on for 12 miles north of central London — then at least the self-enforced exile from my old home in Battersea wouldn't seem so radical. It was one of the factors that clinched my decision to buy.

It turned out to be wishful thinking. Once I moved in I discovered there were no Routemasters running on Chase Side. What the errant example had been doing on that warm Saturday afternoon I never found out, but

presumably it was on learner duty, or possibly preserved. As far as I was concerned it might as well have been sent expressly to inveigle me into this leafy corner of suburbia.

Instead, I had to content myself with DMS-class Leyland Fleetlines on my two local routes, the 135 and the 231. These were to the late 'quiet pack' B20 design, which in most people's book meant they were subjectively noisier than standard Fleetlines, emitting a mournful wail. At least the ones at Enfield benefited from white relief around the upper-deck windows — a concession somewhat inconsistently allowed by garages in other parts of the capital.

Confluence

Enfield Town, just one district of the much bigger London borough of the same name, is a traditional Victorian town centre a mile to the west of the A10 — the last population centre going north before you hit clear open countryside. It's a terminal point for various bus routes coming out of London through Wood Green and Palmers Green, and for others coming in towards London from separate population centres further north.

It's also a transit point, particularly for routes running east-west between places such as Chingford and Barnet. And, in addition, there's been a long-standing practice of routeing certain north-south buses away from the A10 on an extraordinary dog-leg diversion. The 231 was the classic example, passing west though the town centre, turning north up Chase Side, then switching eastwards again at the top end and wending its way back towards the A10.

Where do the buses go?

I wish I could tell you more about bus routes in Enfield Town, but you'll have to indulge me. When I arrived here in 1980 — an exile from central London, but actually a displaced Geordie — I marvelled at picturesque-sounding destinations such as 'Upshire', 'Brimsdown' and 'Carterhatch'. I take no pride in saying this, but I have never knowingly been to Upshire in my life, and in fact I still have only a vague idea where it is. Carterhatch I can handle better; it's a bit more local to me, and it's really just a road.

The point is that even if you're an enthusiast, you don't necessarily take in the totality of a bus network — not unless that's your special interest. You learn about routes that you need to know. So I found out about the 29 (now 329) and the W2, which got me part-way into London; the 307 and 121 to Oakwood, my nearest bona fide Underground station; and the 231, which dropped me off quite near my house. The rest remained much more of a mystery.

I exaggerate, of course, but I'm sure you get my drift. Less relevant routes formed part of the colour and texture of the locality — providing a changing parade of vehicles and liveries to marvel at as the years passed by.

The far north

One of the most marvel-worthy things in Enfield Town was in fact the group of routes that lunged off to northern climes. London Country ran various services north from

Enfield, including the 310 to Hertford. What was more remarkable was that it was joined by the red bus 310A to Hertford and 310B to Harlow — commercially-operated services, run mostly with double-deckers.

The sight of these full-sized red buses so far away from the borders of London has never ceased to amaze me. They tended to follow the ribbon of population development up the A10 axis through places such as Cheshunt, so they were not such rural services as they appeared. Nevertheless, tracts of open country separated some of the townships they served.

Opposite above:
Routemasters were one of Enfield's now-vanished attractions. RM5 heads through the town centre on the long trek to Victoria in 1985.

Opposite below:
Before urban midibuses became an everyday sight around Britain, London Transport used ECW-bodied Bristol LHs on a number of suburban services. These included the W9 in Enfield.

Above:
The W9 was among the first routes to be put out to tender. This 1985 view shows it being operated by an Eastern National Bedford. At that time Eastern National was still part of the National Bus Company, as emphasised by the NBC logo on the front.

More recently, the original green-bus 310 service turned red under the guise of the Lea Valley identity, then Arriva; and single-deckers such as Ikarus-bodied DAFs have been drafted in. Still, the basic structure of the routes remains as I write, along with double-deckers to run on them.

Routemasters after all

Although I was fooled about Routemasters back on my first day in Chase Side, there were Routemasters in Enfield Town in 1980. They were running on the famous route 29, an epic trek all the way out from Victoria via Whitehall, Camden Town, Manor House, Harringay, Wood Green and Winchmore Hill. But they stopped short of Chase Side, terminating at Little Park Gardens, a small neat bus station on the edge of Enfield Town centre.

Not all buses ran right through from end to end, but many did so right up to late evening, and the service had an impressive frequency for most of the day. It's hard to imagine what whim would have persuaded anyone other than an ardent enthusiast to travel the whole length of the route in one sitting, but I'll confess to having done so myself a couple of times. On a more practical level, there were many occasions when I would take a tube out of London as far as Wood Green, then pick up a Routemaster on the 29 for the rest of the journey home.

Short-wheelbase RMs were the standard issue for the

route, and included RM5 (numerically the first standard Routemaster), which was still a regular on the service in the late 1980s, and survives with Arriva as I write this 10 years later. Because of the high frequency and length of the route, they would often gather in twos or even threes at Little Park Gardens, implying a greater density of RM activity than there really was.

Routemaster operation lasted until the first week of November 1988 — surviving (briefly) into an era of half-hearted route-branding. Their withdrawal led to the debut of Leyland Titans in Enfield Town. These were provided by London Northern, and for a while they ran on the route alongside Metrobuses supplied by Leaside Buses. The long route was finally severed in the 1990s, when it was divided into two overlapping segments. The 29 survives at the London end, but in Enfield we are left with a curtailed 329.

Twilight of the 29

Routemaster operation on the 29 had become such a distinctive feature of the landscape that for months before withdrawal I plotted a scheme to video the phenomenon. The only problem — I had no video camera, and ended up rushing out and buying one two days before the Routemasters ran their last journey. So I had just one free afternoon to do the videoing. What you might call a sharp learning curve.

I started shooting in earnest at about half past one. After taking a few scene-setting shots of the buses around Enfield Town, I decided to work my way down the route to central London, stopping wherever I could to take more shots. I got to Wood Green in three hops, actually using Routemasters for the travelling. Then I caught a series of tube trains from one potential location to the next. Hailing the buses while videoing them was an experience in itself. Twice I had to hold the camera in my right hand and stick my left hand out; and each time I felt the dubious glare of a driver who clearly doubted the sincerity of my intention to board.

I later had to rush up four lots of tube station escalators — mostly two steps at a time in a lung-shattering sprint. My problem was that it would be dark by about half-past four, so the whole endeavour had to be crammed into three amazingly eventful hours. By the end of this time I'd taken shots in about a dozen locations, including Charing Cross Road, Trafalgar Square and Victoria. I even tried photographing outwards through the downstairs front window. 'Are they going to put one in Westminster Abbey?' came the booming enquiry from an American lady with a child strapped on her back. 'Buried straight up?'

The Ailsa saga

Back in the mid-1980s, after years of uniformity in the fleets of London Transport and then London Buses, experimentation and economy were in the wind. One of the more bizarre manifestations of this was a decision by London Buses to buy an entire batch of 50 front-engined Volvo Ailsa double-deckers acquired new by the West Midlands PTE in the late 1970s.

Many found themselves allocated to Potters Bar garage (more recently owned by London Northern and Metroline), and they became a familiar sight in Enfield. They were seen particularly on the route W8, linking Chase Farm Hospital with Enfield Town and other local communities, although they also appeared on other routes such as the 310 group. For about four years their high-pitched axle whine and turbocharger whistle echoed round Lavender Hill and Lancaster Road.

They were joined by other London oddities, including some Ailsas from Sheffield with Irish-built bodies by Van Hool McArdle. There were also three further A-registration

Ailsas, in this case new to London. These were eight years younger than the rest and bore more modern R-type Alexander bodies. They included the one-off experimental model with front and rear doors and staircases at both ends.

To add yet further interest, the W8 was also graced with some non-standard second-hand Metrobuses, including single-door examples from operators such as Tyne & Wear — some with Mark II bodywork (virtually unheard-of elsewhere in London at the time). Clearly the world was changing.

Route tendering

When I came to Enfield, buses were either red or green. Most services through the town were run by London Buses, but in the early years London Country was much in evidence too. Apart from the operations north up the A10, it also operated the long-established route 313, which ran westwards from Chingford to Enfield, then turned north up the Ridgway and out into the country, terminating at Potters Bar.

Mainstays on these routes for many years were a batch of MCW-bodied Leyland Atlanteans, which were later augmented by Alexander panoramic-windowed

Opposite:
Sampsons briefly operated LT tendered routes. An ex-London Fleetline loads for Upshire in 1986.

Above:
While most of Eastern National's LT services were operated by small buses, it did have some double-deck contracts. These were initially operated by Bristol VRTs, an unlikely type to find on a London bus service.

versions drafted in from the south. After them came Roe-bodied Leyland Olympians. Their NBC green livery outlasted that of many former NBC companies, though with the coming of London Country North East a crisp new two-tone green and white scheme was eventually adopted. Later a rather less inspired dark green and cream replaced this.

The red bus routes were run almost exclusively by Metrobuses, with the exception of the W9 — a suburban midibus route running south to Winchmore Hill, which was operated by Bristol LH single-deckers.

Then came route tendering. Sudden incomers included Eastern National, providing squat Wadham Stringer-bodied Bedford midis on the W9 down through Grange Park; and Sampsons, a local coach business, which put refurbished blue Fleetlines on the 217B to Upshire (wherever that was). These ended up symbolising the less attractive side of deregulation — smart and distinctive when they first appeared, but dowdy and neglected-looking when the contract was ceded a few years later.

The 313 passed to Grey-Green, which ran a remarkable variety of double- and single-deckers on the route during the 1990s. They became almost as familiar as the London Country buses had been before them.

Another high-profile tendered service was the east-west 307 between Brimsdown and Barnet. Eastern National won this, and ran it for some years with Bristol VRTs; then the company was divided, and the new

Thamesway unit took over with rather sombre maroon and yellow ECW-bodied Olympians, plus some rare new Optare-bodied examples. But by 1996 Leaside (now Arriva) had won the route — now run (like so many) with Dennis Darts.

Opposite above:
After privatisation the London area operations of Eastern National were split off to form part of the new Thamesway company. The driver of a Thamesway ECW-bodied Olympian converses with a Metrobus driver.

Opposite below:
London Country North East used this livery for a short period. A one-time Greater Glasgow Atlantean loads in Enfield centre in 1987.

Above:
Not all London Metrobuses had MCW bodies. This unusual Alexander-bodied example had been new to the West Yorkshire PTE.

Above:
Vehicle shortages and delayed deliveries often saw unusual buses appearing on LT contracts for short periods of time. Grey-Green bought a number of Metrobuses from South Yorkshire Transport, some of which were put into service in their previous owner's colours.

Right:
Little Park Gardens bus station with two buses which were seen as great rivals at the start of the 1980s: the Leyland Titan and MCW Metrobus. Both are on the erstwhile Routemaster route to central London, the 29.

Below right:
A surprise purchase by London Buses was a batch of Ailsas from West Midlands. They had Alexander bodies.

Above:
A former London Country Leyland Olympian in County Bus & Coach's Lea Valley operation.

Above:
Metrobuses were the dominant type in Enfield in the late 1980s and early 1990s. A Leaside Buses example loads while a Grey-Green bus waits to get to the stop. Grey-Green briefly used white, orange and brown as its livery, before adopting a more appropriate grey and green. This is a 1989 view.

Bunching games

Not long after I came to Enfield, the routes running up Chase Side (my local main road) were rejigged. The 231 between Wood Green and Carterhatch remained, but the old 135 was replaced by the 191 between Lower Edmonton and Brimsdown. The Fleetlines also disappeared, to be replaced by Metrobuses; and these were regulars on both routes for most of the 1980s and 1990s.

Neither service was particularly frequent (a 20min headway was deemed generous in those days), but frequently two Metrobuses would be seen moving in sedate convoy down Chase Side, one from each route.

It became a private game with me to look out for three Metrobuses together, but I can honestly say that in the entire era of the Metrobuses I only ever witnessed this phenomenon once. And don't ask me for the photograph; even I don't carry a camera every waking moment, merely in the hope of catching an event that will come only once in 20 years. The only other real excitement was on the rare occasions when alien buses from other routes were diverted up Chase Side for one reason or another. Pointless really to get excited about something so mundane and wholly explicable, but it has always added an exotic touch to the scene.

All this has changed now. In the late 1990s service 191 — latterly a Leaside operation — was put out to tender as a midibus route, and was won by what is now FirstGroup's Thamesway unit. It opted for Dennis Darts in a cheerful lilac and yellow livery (now red and yellow). Wonder of wonders, the frequency was increased to 10min, producing the best service in the area in all my years there. London Northern's 231 struggled on with (usually empty) Metrobuses, but then in 1998 it was also converted to Darts — in this case with bodies by Marshall — and it now terminated at Enfield Chase station, at the south end of Chase Side. With the takeover by Metroline, these have now gained blue relief in corporate style.

So my home run was down to one route. Ironically, though, the high frequency of the 191 means that nowadays it is quite commonplace to see two buses from the same service travelling in convoy along Chase Side, and I've seen three together on many occasions. One of these days it'll happen when I've got my camera with me. I know it will.

Above left:
Access for less able travellers clearly wasn't an issue when this 1982 ECW-bodied Tiger appeared on service in Enfield with County Bus & Coach in 1991.

Left:
MTL London operated DAF single-deckers north from Enfield to Hertford. This example leaving Enfield's bus station has Optare Delta bodywork.

Bottom left:
When Cowie acquired Leaside it added yellow relief and, on some buses, the Cowie logo. This is an early Dennis Dart with the original Dartline style of body, built first by Duple and then by Carlyle.

The present day

It's easy to ignore what is permanently around you. Metrobuses more than any other vehicle type have characterised Enfield for most of the time I've been here, and as I write they survive on several routes. Yet I can't help feeling I've been somehow neglectful of them — perhaps blaming them for not being Routemasters. And presumably they won't last many years more.

Otherwise, more and more routes through Enfield are now run by single-deckers — mostly Dennis Darts; and on the 191 at least, they have undeniably brought improved service levels. And Arriva red livery is creeping in, both on former Leaside buses and on those of the Lea Valley remnant of London Country North East.

The only new double-deckers seen here for many years have been some impressive-looking East Lancs-bodied Dennis Arrows on the W8 along Baker Street and Lancaster Road. Capital Citybus recently won the route from what was latterly MTL London Northern, and the Arrows reflect its final red and yellow livery, now with FirstGroup lettering.

In the long run, will double-deckers survive here at all? I hope so; they seem to add an air of urban substance to the place. Some of the routes are still quite heavily trafficked, and anti-car propaganda may work in their favour.

Besides, in spirit they're the successors to the bus that brought me here in the first place.

Below:
Before the adoption of corporate Arriva colours, some of the vehicles operated by County Bus & Coach in Greater London received a cream and red livery, as shown on this Lea Valley Leyland Olympian.

Bottom:
Capital Citybus is the most recent arrival in Enfield, here operating a one-time London Transport Metrobus in the company's predominantly red livery which was first introduced for buses running on LT contracts in central London. Since being acquired by FirstGroup in 1998 the stylised C logos alongside the destination display have been replaced by the FirstGroup f-logo.

Tellygraphic Memory

The Liver Birds gave a constant update on the Mersey scene as borrowed VRTs and Atlanteans in green became borrowed Dominators in North Western red and blue.

Hero of the Industry

Harry Blundred who found he could replace 40 VRTs with 100 Ford Transits and make money: 3-2-1!

Agony

Plot complexity hit a new high with this sitcom. From making a solid coach, Ward moved into building ersatz Seddon RUs, went bust, the designs were sold off to the Greater London Enterprise Board apparently as Routemaster replacements; however, one coach was completed by a Scottish independent, the company re-emerged as AEC but was immediately sued by BL for brand-name infringement, changed its name to ACE, built a handful of vehicles which failed to convince buyers that ACE was a better home for fleet orders than Ward, went under, somehow re-emerged as Kirn building a prototype Polish citybus… Not even an agony aunt or a dysfunctional psychiatrist could have survived this dizzy whirl.

Casualty

It's grim. It's inevitable. And we've seen it all before. But the crowds want more of the same and the old cast has been brought back to Workington Central for a whole new series. No one builds set pieces like Leyland, so sit back in front of National 2 and watch the events unfold, the protagonists move across the board like chess pieces, the coincidences starting to mount, the customers deserting in droves. A fine workmanlike job, National 2 didn't make a drama out of a driveline (unlike its predecessor) but ultimately it lost the ratings war to Olympian (and to Metrobus from the other side) as the punters went double-deck crazy.

The Young Ones

Once in every lifetime comes a love like this! Get out of here, dull old Supreme and Dominant — make way for youth! Yes, Citizens, we are going to pay twice as much for coaches which will depreciate thrice as quickly — coaches with names like Van Rooijen, Ajokki, Padane and Drogmoeller — but there will be washrooms for everyone and complimentary coffee all round! Hit it, Cliff!

The Word

Deregulation.

Butterflies

We would like a National replacement and it must seat 50-plus. Sorry, the Lynx is too big. No, no, the Tiger Cub is too Danish. We would prefer a Lynx underframe rather than an integral. Actually, six Lynx integrals would do nicely. Make that 200. Hang on, can you fit a different engine? And our own choice of body? (Collapse of stout industry.)

The Price Is Right

In the late 1980s, Scania found a great way of securing market share. Given that tenders were being offered on very short lead-times and DPTAC vehicles were scarce, Scania built numbers of stock vehicles which sat at dealers, awaiting the call 'Mr Availability, Come On Down!' Instant access and favourable exchange rates saw Scania build a wide customer base until a high pound — and some gearbox problems — had a countering effect.

Top Gear

You know (pause) top gear was always dodgy in minibuses. The Mercedes L.608 set your teeth on edge; (pause) once in top, the Sherpa would never change back down; (longer pause) and the City Pacer would fail to get up anything steeper than a 1 in 300 without first consulting its horoscope and slaughtering a goat. (Raise eyebrow.) And none of them had a 0 to 60 time worthy of mention.

GLE EYED
3: 1980s
Individuality Is In

1980s vehicles are much less complex than previously, with turbochargers, encapsulated engines and kneeling Nationals kicked out in favour of leaf springs and four-cylinder breadvans.

Below:
AGONY:
Ward started well, building coaches like this Dalesman seen with Yarranton of Tenbury Wells when new.

Above:
CASUALTY:
The punters went double-deck crazy, although perhaps not for this one. It's a Falcon V in Nottingham.

ALL *CHANGE* in the *West Midlands*

Alistair Douglas looks at the early days of the West Midlands Passenger Transport Executive, set up in October 1969 and taking over four municipal bus operations running over 2,000 buses — Birmingham, Walsall, West Bromwich and Wolverhampton. The PTE subsequently took over part of Midland Red's business, and also the Coventry Corporation bus fleet.

Above:
The Birmingham City Transport fleet was highly standardised, with Daimler Fleetlines progressively replacing a large fleet of half-cab Daimlers, Crossleys and Guys with their distinctive new-look fronts and straight staircases. The PTE had not been long established when some of the earlier ex-Birmingham buses were drafted in to the surrounding towns to replace older buses. A former Birmingham Guy/Metro-Cammell is seen in Wolverhampton in April 1970 alongside a native Guy, an Arab V also bodied by Metro-Cammell. The ex-Birmingham Guy had a 22-year operating life, whereas the ex-Wolverhampton bus had a service life of 12 years.
All photographs by the author

Above:

Single-deckers accounted for only a small part of the Birmingham fleet — in sharp contrast to the situation pertaining 30 years later. These included some lightweights: a dozen Ford R192s bodied by Strachans. This is the Bull Ring in 1974 with two popular cars of the period, a Hillman Avenger and a Morris Marina. New in 1967, the Fords ran with the PTE until 1977.

Below:

Earlier unusual single-deckers were 24 Marshall-bodied Fleetlines. New in 1965, one is seen at the Bull Ring in 1978 operating the Centrebus service which had been inaugurated in 1972 using van-based minibuses.

Above:
Walsall operated a big fleet of little Fleetlines, with a short front overhang. Originally single-door buses (with the door behind the front axle), the PTE added a narrow entrance in the front overhang to make them suitable for one-man operation. The bodywork was by Northern Counties. The bus in the background is a former Walsall Corporation Bedford SBO converted into a mobile canteen.

Left:
The absorption of the Walsall transport undertaking made West Midlands the only trolleybus-operating PTE, with this 1954 Willowbrook-bodied Sunbeam being among the most modern. It was photographed in April 1970. Trolleybus operation came to an end six months later.

Above:

A number of Walsall's older buses had full-width cabs, as illustrated by a 1953 Leyland Titan PD2 with Roe bodywork built on Park Royal frames.

Above:

Three ex-London RTLs saw service with WMPTE but were withdrawn without being repainted in PTE colours. They came with the varied Walsall fleet, which had acquired them in 1959. The OLD registration seems apt.

Right:
Guys were built in Wolverhampton, and the Corporation generally supported its local manufacturer. This 1965 Arab V has Strachans bodywork.

Below:
There were some normal buses in Walsall, such as this Daimler CVG6 with 65-seat Metro-Cammell body. This is Walsall bus station in July 1970 with the Daimler freshly repainted in PTE colours.

Above:
Many of Wolverhampton's Arabs had fully-fronted Metro-Cammell bodies, not unlike those being built on Leyland Titan chassis for Ribble at around the same time. This is a 1961 bus; later batches of Arabs had conventional half-cabs.

Below:
Between 1948 and 1950 Wolverhampton purchased Daimlers as well as Guys. This CVG6 with Brush body retains Wolverhampton livery but sports WMPTE fleetnames. It was withdrawn in this condition in 1971.

Opposite above:
West Bromwich used a distinctive two-tone blue and cream livery with full lining-out, as demonstrated in July 1970 by a Daimler CVG6/30 with Metro-Cammell body. This smart bus had been an exhibit at the 1958 Commercial Motor Show at Earls Court.

Opposite below:
In pursuit of service integration the PTE purchased a large part of the Midland Red business in December 1973, adding 413 buses to its fleet. Many of these were Midland Red's own-build BMMO models, including this S17 in central Birmingham in April 1974.

Below:
Local government reorganisation in April 1974 saw Coventry fall within the area of the new West Midlands council, and the city's 308-strong bus fleet was taken over by the PTE. Most Coventry buses were Daimlers. This is a CVG6 with Metro-Cammell Orion bodywork, photographed in September 1974 after being transferred to Dudley.

BUSES & BAGPIPES

Robert E. Jowitt, having pursued buses round much of Western Europe for close on 40 years, turns his attention belatedly to the buses — and other charms — of the Athens of the North.

Close encounter. A Volvo Olympian coming in from South St Andrew Street jostles for the Princes Street lights with a Lothian open-top Atlantean. All photographs by the author

The sea mist, which had been thickening gradually as the train sped north across Northumberland, thinned for a moment to allow a decent view of the Royal Border Bridge and the town of Berwick Upon Tweed and then, as we crossed the border past that iron sign which had been familiar to me from schoolboy railway books since my childhood, the greyness swirled ever closer about the track, so I wondered how much of Scotland I would see.

It had been hazy when I caught the train from Knaresborough in the morning, and sunny in the early afternoon when I caught another train on from York and still sunny as the train traversed the viaducts at Durham and Newcastle upon Tyne — and then the mist started to gather and by the time the train arrived in Edinburgh it was pretty thick.

At Waverley station I was met by my host, my second cousin. It may come as something of a shock to those readers familiar with my writings and habits, such as sampling taverns and photographing unknown young ladies in the streets of strange cities with a bus or tram in the background as an excuse, to learn that my second cousin is a Reverend Canon of the Episcopalian Church, retired only a few years ago from the Edinburgh Episcopalian Cathedral, the spires of which were about to be included in my photographs of Edinburgh girls and buses, with a bit of luck and a bit less mist.

I could add that the previous night, being in the way of catching up with second cousins, I had been the guest of another second cousin whom I had not seen for 20 years, this one living near Knaresborough — hence the train thence — being also a second cousin of my Edinburgh cousin and, as another item to startle my readers, at one time High Sheriff of Yorkshire.

But there, even the best families, counting Canons and High Sheriffs in their generations, now and then produce black sheep who instead of adopting a respectable profession choose to waste their time in Bohemian pursuits such as photographing trams and buses and girls in the streets, which is what I have been doing since I first started on the antique trams of Paderborn in Germany — at that moment because I could not find any picture postcards of them — 40 years bar a couple of months before I first set foot in Edinburgh.

Below:

The piper homeward plods his weary way — in company with a suitably-clad lassie and a decidedly un-Scottish dog — while an immaculate Lothian Leyland National waits for the lights at the west end of Princes Street.

Lisbon. With TRAMS. Edinburgh, having scrapped trams before I started photographing them, could not claim a high place in my list of destinations.

Nevertheless, in more recent years, I was honoured to be asked to join an elite band by the name of Fotobus, whose members take photographs of buses in more unusual vein than the three-quarter front record shot. I have to admit that some of my attitudes — and photographs — raise an eyebrow and provoke some controversy even among these forward-looking gentlemen, but, be that as it may, the members of Fotobus, in moving the site of the AGM from one interesting city to another, proposed in politeness to their esteemed Scottish members that the 1998 AGM should take place in Edinburgh, a proposal which, with my Episcopalian cousin's invitation in mind, I eagerly seconded.

Thus I arrived in Edinburgh, to be greeted by my cousin and the mist. My cousin apologised for the mist, told me it is known as the haar, this being a Scottish East Coast word for a Scottish East Coast sea mist, and hoped, though without much conviction in his tone, that it would clear in the course of my five-day visit; and drove me via various landmarks which I was soon to know well to his comfortable tenement in Marchmont.

Let me here say that no black sheep could have a better welcome or more hospitable treatment than I had from my cousin the Canon, who did not in the least resent my spending hours traipsing the streets to photograph buses — and, as he must have guessed, for he knew my works, girls in front of the buses — and would feed me at whatever hour I staggered back to Marchmont after half a dozen promenades along Princes Street and diverse deviations on either side. Whereafter we would wallow in family history over half a dozen or more generations and a glass or two of port, and discussions on the diverse and numerous architectural gems I had encountered in the course of my wanderings.

The architectural gems are perhaps most crowded together or at least visible, the haar permitting, in the offing or slightly beyond, if you start out on a perambulation from the eastern end of Princes Street. In a few yards along here you can see more than half of the subjects of Edinburgh picture postcards, with the National Monument on the top of Calton Hill, the Post Office, the Register House, Wellington's Statue, the North British Hotel and the Scott Monument, while on the far side of North Bridge are the offices of the Scotsman on one side of the road and an equally splendid Victorian jewel on the other, the Carlton Highland Hotel, and westwards, spread densely up the steep hillside, the picturesque ancient many-floored high houses of the Old Town.

Then up St Andrews Street is St Andrews Square, one of the main delights of the Edinburgh New Town of the 18th century — and of the city's bus station, although few would claim that to be a delight. Back in Princes Street is Jenner's department store in high fin de siècle baroque with goddesses worthy of the Paris Opera, to which when it, Jenner's, was new I dare say the good citizens of Edinburgh objected as much as I do now to some of its

Top:
Above and beyond, a Lothian Olympian crosses the North Bridge, while below and in front an ex-Nottingham veteran waits on the Waverley Bridge.

Above:
The merits of the Scottish Socialist Alliance are enumerated to potential female supporters while a First bus with traditional Scottish destination blind layout leads a mixture of old and new vehicles along Princes Street.

Why had I never been to Edinburgh before? I had been to Glasgow three times: once in tramway days, once on the last tramway day, and again when there were still trolleybus days, as you might say, though after that I had never returned. The truth of the matter is that, though I had an open invitation from my cousin from a quarter of a century back — even before he was a Canon — I was wont to travel, when I could travel at all, to places like

more recent and shoe-box-like neighbours. And opposite the goddesses the Scott Monument towers up 200ft, but I am no better informed on the delights of this than ever I was by picture postcards, for during my visit the Scott Monument remained shrouded in scaffolding.

Anyway, hemmed in by all this splendour and through its midst, there comes — and goes — an almost ceaseless string of buses, and by 'almost ceaseless' I mean to say that there is never a moment when there is no bus in sight and often you can see a dozen or more at once; and even for a tram lover like me this quantity of buses in this quality of surroundings is a great delight.

However, at least so far as the newer vehicles are concerned, I am as ill informed as I am on the finer details of the Scott Monument. I can see that the majority are Lothian and sport the lovely maroon livery formerly so excellent a feature of Edinburgh Corporation buses and trams. Among the relatively infrequent single-decks I can recognise the Leyland Nationals and choose to dismiss the rest as box-like modernity, while for the double-decks I lean on the knowledge of Gavin Booth, lifelong Edinburgh citizen and well known as a former editor of Buses Annual.

Mr Booth tells me that, apart from the Atlanteans, which I can identify myself and of which more in a moment, the older double-deckers have ECW bodywork

and the next generation is Alexander R-type on Leyland Olympian chassis which subsequently and with little outward change becomes Volvo chassis and with the newest deliveries the body is the Alexander Royale.

Looking at my photographs after the event I do become aware of these differences, just as I become aware, over 40 years of study, of subtle variations in the Paderborn trams, but while I am on the spot and with numerous other distractions I merely subconsciously register the various types.

Then turning from the Lothian buses to the interurban interlopers I observe that these, presumably all formerly Scottish something-or-other, are now all FirstBus; and while most if not all their double-deckers are identical or similar to the Lothian buses, though far more luridly liveried, there are frequent incursions by some excellently antiquated single-deckers. These are Seddon Pennines, with registration numbers from the 1980s, but of a type

Below:
As the celebrated silhouette of Edinburgh Castle emerges from the haar and a large seagull settles on the head of a cavalry hero, a Lothian Volvo Olympian roars east along Princes Street.

introduced in the early 1970s, and with an Alexander body which first appeared with stunning modernity in the early 1960s — about the time when the last Paderborn trams died — and which by sheer brilliance of design manages to look both thoroughly roadworthy and desirably preservable more than 30 years later.

A lot more of yesterday's bus history, if now mutilated by several different types of open-topping, is foregathered on the Waverley Bridge and close below the Scott Monument, in the form of the Lothian Edinburgh sightseeing tours and the rival Guide Friday Edinburgh sightseeing tours. I assume that the Lothian vehicles, regardless of transmogrifications, are local; but the Guide Fridays, like those in Bath or Stratford-upon-Avon, might have sprung from anywhere. Not that the tourists will know or care…

But this spot on the corner of the Waverley Bridge has obvious lucrative tourist-trapping potential, and there is always a bagpiper, though not always the same one, every time I pass, shrilling laments or pibrochs or other Scottish airs, and then, westwards along Princes Street and hardly beyond the skirl of the pipes on the Waverley Bridge, the pipes are shrilling again by the Royal Scottish Academy.

Now, on the south side of Princes Street, opens the great trough of the West Princes Street Gardens, worth a

steep descent and an even steeper climb back afterwards (or so it feels) for the sake of viewing a splendid fountain decorated with mildly improper gilt nymphs, again in 19th century Parisian style. Beyond the trough rises the precipitous crag crowned by the Castle. This is so well known on picture postcards, shortbread tin lids, calendars and other publications that I think it unnecessary to add any description of it, save to say it makes a fine backdrop for the hordes of buses racing along Princes Street, looking very impressive with the haar swirling about it, and equally impressive later on in brilliant sunshine.

For on my second afternoon the sun comes through, and the next couple of days produce a heatwave of Mediterranean proportions.

Continuing the perambulation westwards towards the Episcopalian spires, we reach the end of Princes Street. Just round the corner is the Caledonian Hotel (the Caledonian Railway having in happier days its terminus here) and this, though not quite so ebullient in style as the North British Hotel, is grand enough. West of here is a rather elegant quarter of substantial 18th century dwellings with the Episcopalian Cathedral of St Mary in their midst. The Cathedral, built in the 1870s, is regarded as one of Sir Gilbert Scott's noblest essays in Early Pointed Gothic. The buses in this quarter seem to travel rather sedately.

Above:
Greyfriars Bobby, the canine hero of Edinburgh, sits on his pedestal on the corner of George IV Bridge and Candlemaker Row while the passers-by seem more intent on the living example of doggery. No one pays any attention to the Atlantean behind which, on the nearside anyway, is reasonably normal.

Right:
Guide Friday and Lothian open-tops with an enormous aggregate age and amazing variety in bodywork detail queue for custom on Waverley Bridge with new and old in airport transportation beyond and the mist over the Old Town in the background. Meanwhile, midway, pedal power prevails.

South of the Caledonian Hotel begins a somewhat less salubrious area, with broad streets of Victorian tenements — interspersed at intervals with daring examples of modern architecture — along which the buses hurtle with almost tramcar-like zest, perhaps because it is the kind of district you would expect to find trams (or would have expected) and perhaps the maroon livery adds to the aura.

Back along Princes Street. Every time I walk along Princes Street — and as I have implied already it is several times a day — the pavements are always thronged with girls. All this makes as good a foreground to the buses as the Castle makes a background.

Now if I say that when you have seen one Edinburgh girl you have seen them all, this is in no way intended as an insult; far from it, because many of them are extremely attractive, but a great many of them have the same sort of beauty as the next, oval-faced with wide mouths and high cheek bones. They are as distinctive a type as the famous Arlesiennes in Provence.

The buses, at least the double-deckers, are mostly pretty similar too, most of them being quite a lot younger

Above left:
A Lothian National passing St John's Highland Kirk in the Lawnmarket. This church was until recent years noted for holding a Sunday service in Gaelic, but the service now takes place elsewhere and the building is used for secular purposes by the festival.

Above:
Nosing along the Royal Mile with a mist-shrouded St Giles Cathedral in the background, an Atlantean clearly displays the inharmonious arrangement of lower- and upper-deck windows on the off-side.

than the girls, except the Atlanteans, which must be not that far short of 20, but the Atlanteans seem not to be allowed along Princes Street...too old, perhaps, except I observe one on driver training. But by the Royal Scottish Academy, back in the sound of the skirl of the pipes again, the Atlanteans dart across Princes Street from north to south, and south to north too, up Hanover Street, graced very suitably at the top by a statue of George IV on a tall column.

103

This street is also graced by some of the last of the Atlanteans with the curious arrangement of the pillars of the upper deck windows not being in line with those of the lower deck. Even I, largely ignorant of modern and not quite so modern buses, know that this is something quite peculiar and decidedly Scottish. These are actually sufficiently unmodern that apparently they are very shortly to be withdrawn.

From the statue of George IV and parallel to Princes Street runs George Street, east and west. This, served not by Atlanteans but by Leyland Nationals and more modern buses and something called Routemaster which proves to be a minibus, is the principal thoroughfare of the 18th century New Town, but its gracious architecture is not improved by dense lines of parked automobiles throughout its length. The same applies to Hanover Street and the other streets which lead from Princes Street to George Street, but on the other hand they boast convenient bars in cellars with a useful array of Scottish ales.

Thus refreshed I can start south from Princes Street, past the classical columns of the Royal Scottish Academy and then immediately afterwards the classical columns of the National Gallery — which in baking heat add a lot to Edinburgh's claim to being The Athens of the North — to climb the fearsome hill to the Old Town. With my last gasp I reach the Royal Mile or that bit of it known as the Lawn Market and collapse into a strategically placed tavern in which I take a Belgian lager, this in view of my hill-climbing exertion and the heat, both Lisbon-like, in default of any Portuguese-type beer. Being strategically placed means also that it affords a view of Atlanteans. As it lies on a fairly direct line from Princes Street to Marchmont I actually call in more than once.

Above:
A Lothian Leyland Olympian halted below the handsome north front of the Caledonian Hotel, a splendid architectural example of the palmy days of railway supremacy.

Left:
An interesting and typical arrangement of gables and chimneys on the east side of St Patrick's Square, with a profile of a Lothian Olympian as a foreground.

From this point one can — and I do — go up to the Castle or down to St Giles Cathedral and, opposite, the City Chambers, where I see four fire engines assemble with much verve and dash, though there does not appear to be a fire to put out, merely a couple of buses to delay.

Leaving the picturesque high old houses of the Royal Mile behind and proceeding from the tavern — it is called after someone who did something wicked like murder but I can't remember who or what — in a straight ahead or southerly or Marchmont direction the road appears to be level, but then suddenly you look over a wall and see a road a long way down below, and the ground floor next to you is also the third floor (at least) if you are counting from the road below.

This level road is in truth a bridge across a deep narrow valley and is known as George IV Bridge, the floor of the valley being covered almost entirely with these high buildings except where somewhat sinister alleys thread their way through the bottom. They end up in a square known as the Grassmarket, a gem of architectural antiquity and, says my cousin, a mixture of modern chic and old vice. From here a precipitous bus route leads up Candlemaker Row to the south end of George IV Bridge.

On the point between these two is the small but celebrated statue of the small but celebrated dog Greyfriars Bobby; his story of canine devotion is surely too well known to need repetition in this pages. Beyond him the buses fork left; they can't fork right, it's a one-way street so buses only come inwards. The left fork is called Bristo Place, I don't know who Bristo was, for the guide book doesn't say or I don't read it carefully enough, and anyway beyond Bristo Place is Bristo Square which happens to be the terminus of bus route 60.

Now I cannot say I pay greater attention to route 60 than to any other route, but I do notice that the Edinburgh Travelmap ([sic] why one word when two would do?) makes the extraordinary mistake — a Freudian slip perhaps inspired by the increased number of Continental-style eating and drinking dens in these EEC days — of describing this bus terminus as Bistro Square. In the prevailing gastronomic circumstances in this district, close to the University, it is perhaps not so inaccurate…

From this point it is but a short walk to Nicolson Street. Nicolson Street then becomes Clerk Street which turns into South Clerk Street which becomes Newington Road and then Ninto Street and then Mayfield Gardens and then…only I don't follow it further. But it is really all one long and fairly straight road and absolutely abounding in buses and moreover down every side street, or most of them, are lovely glimpses of the great crags of Arthur's Seat all clad in a mantle of bright yellow broom.

Below left:
A fairly elderly Olympian with the rarely photographed but not unimposing Victorian west end of the Castle aloft in the background.

Below right:
Pedal power beats buses eastwards along Princes Street. In the background on the left is the tower of St John's, Princes Street, with the pinnacle of St George's West behind it and the spires of St Mary's Episcopalian Cathedral beyond.

This habit of applying several different names to one road is fairly widespread, but I notice, as I travel down it on a bus, that Leith Walk manages to remain such throughout its length, except for the inner or Edinburgh end being known as Leith Street. It is in Leith Street that I board the bus, along with a young couple with a child and a vacuum cleaner, and the driver bids this family very firmly, on account of the fare they give him — perhaps after the vacuum cleaner it is all the change they have left — that they must descend at such-and-such a stop.

To this they apparently agree, and ascend to the upper deck, but when the bus reaches this point they fail to descend, and the driver first of all shouts at them from his seat and finally comes up to reinforce the message, to be greeted by a torrent of invective as, mostly in four-letter words, an oppressor of the poor. As the oppressor of the poor shows no sign of leaving the upper deck, let alone taking the bus any further, they eventually yield to force majeure and the growls of some of the other passengers. I remain quietly in the front seat during this interlude and, having paid a more adequate fare, am in due time deposited at the end of Leith Walk, where, despite the delay, I am in time for the AGM of Fotobus, which, as may be apparent, is being held in Leith.

There is quite a lot happening in Edinburgh this weekend besides the Fotobus AGM. I gather there is a football match against the Norwegians, and I see two chaps sitting on a bench rather despondently flapping Norwegian flags. I don't know whether they won or lost, but I do know, though I have no interest whatsoever in football, that the Edinburgh local team, Hearts, do win their match. Not, as far as I can gather, against the Norwegians, but anyway it would seem to be their first win against whoever it is in 20 years and I witness them borne in triumph on the top deck of an Edinburgh Sightseeing open-top bus through a dense and adoring throng.

Then, up on the open space known as the Meadows, on my way back to Marchmont, I encounter a large crowd of gents all in black suits and bedecked with ribbons, with a band in attendance and being harangued with a prayer from one of their number on a loud speaker. Enquiry of a policeman — of whom there are several — brings the answer that it is the biennial meeting of the Scottish Orangemen. The loud-speaker, when the prayer is finished, announces that the meeting will now be addressed by the inspired tongue of Someone Mac Someone; he starts his address with an urgent call for an ambulance. Perhaps someone fainted; it is very hot.

I do not stay to find out, or to listen to the inspired words, for all along the fringe of the Meadows is a line of buses which brought the Orangemen hither, many from Glasgow and some of considerable antiquity. The buses, that is.

And then I become aware of further religious concerns. Round and about the Royal Scottish Academy and up and down the hill above it and on the immediate sections of Princes Street with the Leylands and the

Volvos and those lovely Seddons roaring past, among the homeless sitting despairing with dingy dogs on the pavements and the drop-outs sitting on the steps below the columns drinking cans of lager and by the piper standing skirling his pibrochs and among the bare-midriffed lassies there stride several purposeful gentlemen, some laity and some clergy, but all manifestly coming from or going to the same place.

The Assembly of the Church of Scotland has just started. They do not assemble, I think, by means of buses, old or otherwise, and even if they did there would be nothing I could do about it, for though they may remain a week or even a fortnight, it is time for me to have a last glass of port and session of family history with my Episcopalian cousin and then, with the morn, to catch a train south, for England.

And, drat it, to leave behind me another day of brilliant sunshine. It is difficult to believe that the haar ever existed.

Left:
The Meadows are the scene of the biennial assembly of Scottish Orangemen and the coaches and buses which bring them there. At the front is an elderly Marshall of Baillieston coach with, further back, assorted Olympians from SMT and Kelvin Central.

Below:
Hearts borne homeward to their ground in triumph after their great 1998 victory in the Scottish Cup, travelling on a suitably inscribed Lothian Atlantean with attendant fans. And if the fans look this cheerful for a win, what would they be like if their team had lost...?

CLEVELAN

Cleveland Transit was formed in 1974 to take over the operations of Teesside Municipal Transport, itself a relatively young organisation, having been set up in 1968 to unite the bus fleets of Middlesbrough and Stockton corporations and the Teesside Railless Traction Board. Cleveland Transit was taken over by Stagecoach in 1994. Kevin Lane illustrates two decades of Cleveland Transit.

Above:

A busy scene in Stockton High Street in the mid-1970s. In the foreground is a 1960 Leyland Titan PD2 which had been new to Stockton Corporation and was one of that operator's last rear-entrance buses, as from 1961 Stockton bought forward-entrance Titans. It is passing a Daimler Fleetline which had been ordered by Middlesbrough but was in fact delivered new to TMT in 1969. It has a dual-door Northern Counties body and, in line with Middlesbrough policy, a Gardner 6LW engine instead of the standard 6LX. Also visible is another Fleetline and a United Auto Bristol Lodekka. All photographs by the author

Left:

On contract work at Teesport, an ex-TRTB Roe-bodied Titan, unusual in having Cave-Browne-Cave heating, a system more commonly associated with the Bristol Lodekka. New in 1966, it survived with Cleveland Transit until 1980.

CAMERA

Left:
Middlesbrough Corporation was an early convert to the Fleetline and by 1964 was running 30, all with Northern Counties bodies. This 1964 bus was later converted for one-man operation which explains the unusual destination layout alongside the pay-on-entry sign above the driver's windscreen.

Below:
Second-hand Atlanteans were fairly unusual when TMT bought a dozen former Ribble Gay Hostess coaches in 1971. Before entering service they were upseated from 59 to 69, retaining their original coach seats upstairs but having bus seats fitted to the lower saloon. Reseating, which involved removing the rear luggage compartment, was a slow job and the last of these Atlanteans finally entered service in the summer of 1974. They were sold in 1978-9.

Right:

In 1974 Cleveland Transit took over the 22-vehicle operation of Saltburn Motor Services. This was made up mainly of Bedfords, including this battle-scarred 1966 VAM5 with Plaxton body, seen at the rear of Cleveland Transit's Middlesbrough depot (since closed) in 1981. The VAM was withdrawn in 1982.

Below:

In 1975 Cleveland Transit bought four small buses long before they became fashionable. Two were Ford A-series and the other two, one of which is seen here, were Leyland 440EAs. The Leylands had Asco bodies with 19 seats. The location is Guisborough on a former Saltburn Motor Services route.

Above:
As the Fleetline was being phased out, Cleveland Transit started buying Dennis Dominators. A Dominator passes a Fleetline in Norton in the summer of 1994. Both have Northern Counties bodies.

Left:
At the end of the 1980s Cleveland Transit switched to full-size single-deckers, after buying small numbers of minibuses. It took 30 Leyland Lynxes. One is seen in Yarm in 1990.

Below:
In 1988 Cleveland Transit bought this former Southdown Leyland Titan PD3. It is seen on the Stockton-Hardwick-Stockton circular service in the summer of 1994.

Above:
After the Lynxes came a batch of 12 Volvo B10Bs with Plaxton Verde bodies. They were new in 1994 and were the last vehicles to be ordered before the company was bought by Stagecoach. They were in consequence among the last vehicles to be delivered in Cleveland Transit's green, yellow and white colours — although the Cleveland livery was in fact applied to early purchases under Stagecoach ownership.

Below:
The Cleveland Coaches name was introduced for the coach fleet, which included this unusual ECW-bodied Olympian seen heading to Newcastle in 1994. The Cleveland Coaches business was sold to Delta of Stockton in 1995, although this particular vehicle was retained by Cleveland. The Olympian was new to Alder Valley for London commuter operations.

Tellygraphic Memory
That BET Leopard (clearly imported by the Beeb) on Ballykissangel.

Hero of the Industry
Brian Souter, the man with red shoes who made buses respectable on the stock exchange with careful management, high standards, tough goals and high profits.

Blind Date
He was Parisian, mature and confident. She was a true Londoner, living in a big house in Broadway. Their romance had so much going for it but somehow London Buses was never going to have more than a quick French fling despite the cameras clicking away. *Blind Date* normally ends in embarrassment. *Romeo and Juliet* ended in tragedy. The PR100 ended in Scunthorpe.

Peak Practice
The power, the pathos, the human suffering, the constant changes in the line up behind the unchanging title. This one will run and run; a guaranteed smash, with big overseas sales. We'll call it… Olympian.

Changing Rooms
The participants' faces are always a study when they see what they have done in this entertaining DIY game. Sometimes a talented designer pulls off a visual delight and on other occasions, you just know the owner is in for a big disappointment. It's all down to talent, but, let's face it dears, if you insist on fitting all your favourite spares to a previously okay East Lancs body, the odds are that the coachbuilder may be willing, but the end product will be a bit of a shed.

QED
Dennis started with a simple question — what do the customers want? Answer: A medium-sized bus costing £1,000 per seat all in (at 1988 prices). It assembled the most proven components in a cost-effective package. Everyone paused, worried — they had all seen little

miracle buses before (Panther Cub, Seddon RU, DAB Tiger Cub) which despite the right components, never made the big time. But what looks right just sometimes is right — and then they fell upon Dennis like wolves with big cheque books. Quod erat demonstrandum.

Drop The Dead Donkey
Iveco tried so hard with big buses. Nobody cared.

Antiques Roadshow
If you've found one of these in your attic, don't get excited. The Wright Handybus was cheap in 1992 and by jingo it looks it now. Even on delivery it wasn't easy to convince customers that something genuinely new was being used; the utilitarian profile and 1950s-style front look so old-fashioned that any vehicle not fresh from the paintshop appears too old to be in service. Imagine the difficulty of making customers believe you valued them if you had a big fleet of these. Very soon, the Ballymena factory went to the opposite extreme and discovered that style sells — big time.

Wheel of Fortune
There have always been symbiotic relationships between bus builders — AEC and Park Royal, MCW and Scania, Optare and DAF — but the biggest money-spinner in recent years has been that between Plaxton and Dennis. As wheelchair accessibility has come to the fore, so the Dennis Dart has created something approaching a seller's market for the first time in a generation. Most have benefited from the standardised and price-conscious bodies built in Scarborough, but as the Dart has grown, its axleweights and tyre loadings have pushed up to the extent that a 41-seater requires semi-integral construction. And only one builder has won the prize to build what everyone wants — a *fin de siècle* 11m SLF saloon compatible with all those other Darts — the Super Pointer Dart.

They Think It's All Over
And for the moment, so far as British-owned chassis production is concerned, it is now — apart from Dennis.

GLE EYED
4: 1990s
Corporate Image Is In

1990s vehicles are much more complex than previously with turbocharged, encapsulated, kneeling buses as standard.

Below:
PEAK PRACTICE
Olympians of Lothian Region Transport stand enmeshed in the traffic of Edinburgh's Princes Street.

Above:
QED
Greater Manchester Buses North bought Darts with Northern Counties bodies. This one, delivered after GMBN had been taken over by FirstBus, is seen in Ramsbottom.

LONDON *GREEN*

Geoff Mills illustrates some of the variety to be found in the fleet of London Country Bus Services, the successor to London Transport's green country area operations.

Below:

The best-looking half-cab ever? A classic RT-type AEC Regent in Green Line colours on a local service in Harlow. Although this looks like a 1960s picture of a London Transport bus, it was in fact taken in May 1970, shortly after the creation of London Country on 1 January of that year. This 1948 bus was among the oldest vehicles acquired by London Country. It lasted until 1972. The last RTs were withdrawn in 1977.

All photographs in this article by the author

Right:
The first buses to carry London Country fleetnames were XF-class Daimler Fleetlines repainted for operation on Blue Arrow commuter services. These buses had Park Royal bodies.

Above:
Superbus was an early attempt at raising the standards of bus services back in 1972, long before the marketing campaigns and route branding which became commonplace in the late 1980s. Superbus operated in Stevenage in a yellow and blue livery using the three types of vehicle seen here in 1973 — an AEC Swift, a Leyland National and a Metro-Scania. The distinctive livery was phased out at the end of the 1970s.

Left: and below:
London Country inherited an ageing fleet and vehicles were transferred in from other NBC companies, including a batch of 12 new Marshall-bodied Swifts from South Wales Transport in 1971. The first view shows one soon after entering service, with fixed windows, polished mouldings and in London Country's original dark green livery. The second view shows a sister vehicle on the same route 10 years later in all-over NBC leaf green, with the mouldings removed or painted over and with top-sliders added to three of the side windows. And somebody's nicked the AEC badge.

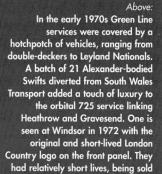

Above:
In the early 1970s Green Line services were covered by a hotchpotch of vehicles, ranging from double-deckers to Leyland Nationals. A batch of 21 Alexander-bodied Swifts diverted from South Wales Transport added a touch of luxury to the orbital 725 service linking Heathrow and Gravesend. One is seen at Windsor in 1972 with the original and short-lived London Country logo on the front panel. They had relatively short lives, being sold in 1979-80.

Above:
Routemaster coaches survived long enough on Green Line operations to be repainted in NBC leaf green. Indeed this one is seen in service in Grays in 1979, by which time Green Line was running real coaches.

Above:
Early Green Line Nationals were buses with NBC's two-colour 'local coach' livery, as seen loading in Brentwood in 1973. At least later Green Line Nationals did sport high-backed seats.

Above:
London Country's first proper coaches were five AEC Reliances with Plaxton Panorama Elite bodies, delivered in 1973 in National white livery. Unusually they carried no fleet numbers — at least not until 1976. One is seen in Victoria coach station running on hire to National Travel (South East) in 1975.

Unusual additions to the fleet, which was made up mainly of Atlanteans, were 15 Bristol VRTs with full-height ECW bodies, easily identifiable by the deep white band above the lower deck windows. They were delivered in 1977 and had Leyland 500-series engines. They were transferred to Bristol Omnibus in 1980.

Between 1973 and 1977 London Country built up a fleet of 67 Bristol LHSs for rural services. They had 35-seat ECW bodies.

Right:
Unusual acquisitions in 1977 were 10 five-year-old AEC Reliances from the large East Midlands independent, Barton Transport. These had Plaxton Panorama Elite bodies with three-plus-two seating for 60 people.

Below:
There was a remarkable change in policy on Green Line services in 1977, with the introduction of 30 AEC Reliances with coach bodies by Duple and Plaxton. By 1979 there would be over 100 — and in 1980 they were joined by the first imported coaches for London Country — two Volvo B58s with Duple bodies. The first is seen at the 1980 Brighton coach rally.

Above:
When Atlantean production
ceased, London Country
turned to the replacement
Olympian model with an
initial batch of 30. Like
some of the Atlanteans
which had preceded them,
the Olympians had Roe
bodies and these were
modified to incorporate
London Country's standard
Park Royal-style
windscreen. Most NBC
Olympians had BET-style
screens, as used on the
ECW bodies fitted to VRTs
and Atlanteans.

Above:
The early 1980s saw London Country Atlanteans operating on London
sightseeing tours. For this work they were repainted red and converted to
open-top. This 1972 bus with Metro-Cammell body came from a batch of
30 which had been diverted from Midland Red.

Above:
It's easy to forget that London Country was among the many operators to buy prematurely-retired London Transport Fleetlines. This 1973 bus was one of seven acquired in 1980. It is seen on training duties at St Albans two years later.

Above:
The upgrading of Green Line services, started in 1977, continued into the 1980s with Leyland Tigers, following the end of AEC Reliance production. This is a 1984 Tiger with high-floor 37-seat Berkhof Everest bodywork for the London to Heathrow Flightline service. London Country also ran Tigers with Duple, Plaxton and ECW coach bodies.

ODD
SINGLES

Most types of bus are built in reasonably large numbers. Billy Nicol searches out some odd single-deckers in recent Scottish operations.

Below:

Converted. Two Volvo B10Ms with Plaxton Derwent bus bodies were bought by Strathclyde's Buses in 1988 — but were subsequently fitted with coach seats and repainted into the company's black, white and orange coach livery, as seen in Linwood in 1994.
All photographs by the author

Above:
Halved. It started life as
a double-decker in
1975 but was rebuilt as
a single-decker 10
years later. Strathclyde
Buses operated this
Ailsa until 1993 when
it was sold to Black
Prince of Morley —
at which point it
transpired that there
were questions about
its legality. It is seen
in Paisley.

Above:
Imported. There was a time when the idea of Hungarian bodywork on a Glaswegian
bus would have seemed like the fevered imaginings of deranged enthusiasts after an
evening in one of the city's hostelries. But it came to pass, when five DAF SB220s
were hired to cover a vehicle shortage in 1992-3 following a major depot fire.

Above:
Famous? Ask a bus enthusiast to name a famous Belgian and alongside Hercule Poirot he may mention Bernard Van Hool. And then again, he may not. Van Hool coach bodies are commonplace in Britain, but bus bodies are rare indeed. This B10M was new to Hutchison of Overtown but later operated for Henderson of Hamilton, between 1991 and 1995. It is seen in East Kilbride.

Above
Continental. Jonckheere, like Van Hool, is best known in Britain for coach bodywork. AA Buses operated three Scania K92s with Jonckheere bus bodies in the early 1990s. They were new to Scancoaches of London, who had bought them for London Transport tendered services

Above:
Utilitarian. Lex built a small number of bus bodies for the National Bus Company, including this angular vehicle which was new to United Counties in 1981. In 1993 it was operating for Shuttle Buses of Kilwinning. It was based on a Bedford YMQ-S chassis.

Left:
Unique. Well, unique in Scotland. This was the only Dennis Domino ever to operate north of the border. It had an Optare body and had been new to the South Yorkshire PTE. It was operated by Stark of Bridge of Weir, trading as Quarriers, and reached Scotland via the fleet of Stevensons of Uttoxeter.

Above:

Rare. Leyland Cubs with Duple Dominant bus bodies were rare indeed, being bought by just two operators — and both of these in Scotland. Lothian Region Transport took 16, Central Scottish took two. One of the Central Cubs is seen later in life with Munro of Uddingston who used it to compete with Central's successor, Kelvin Central. This is a 1994 view in Glasgow's Argyle Street.

Left:

Chopped. Cut-down double-deckers are seldom handsome buses, and this Kelvin Central Fleetline was no exception. It started life in 1978 as a double-decker with Lancashire United Transport. After a low-bridge accident it was rebuilt by Northern Counties (its original builder) in 1986 for LUT's successor, Greater Manchester Transport. Kelvin Central acquired it with the local bus services of Morrow of Clydebank in 1992.